## The**inspirational**series™
#### Overcoming adversity and thriving

# Liar Laurie
## Breaking the Silence on Sexual Assault
### BY LAURIE KATZ

We are proud to introduce The**inspirational**series™. Part of the Trigger family of innovative mental health books, The**inspirational**series™ tells the stories of the people who have battled and beaten mental health issues. For more information visit: www.triggerpublishing.com

# THE AUTHOR

Laurie is an elementary teacher from Boston, Massachusetts who spent her undergraduate years studying early childhood education, then completed a Master's in Education. Her educational background has honed her empathy, adaptability, and human development skills. She has two fur babies and is an avid outdoor runner and amateur chef.

Her life was thrown into turmoil at 18 when she was raped on her third weekend of college. After being told not to go to the police, she navigated her university's hearing process and was silenced. She struggled in silence for years, on the brink of suicide, until she was finally able to get help. Through therapy she has accepted that what happened was not her fault and that her life has value. She is passionate about ending sexual assault on college campuses and elsewhere, and helping to expand the conversation on helpful services for survivors. She is now ready to share her own story and help others in the process.

First published in Great Britain 2018 by Trigger

Trigger is a trading style of Shaw Callaghan Ltd & Shaw Callaghan 23 USA, INC.

The Foundation Centre

Navigation House, 48 Millgate, Newark

Nottinghamshire NG24 4TS UK

www.triggerpublishing.com

Copyright © Laurie Katz 2018

British Library Cataloguing in Publication Data

A CIP catalogue record for this book is available upon request
from the British Library

ISBN: 978-1-912478-75-0

This book is also available in the following e-Book and Audio formats:

MOBI: 978-1-912478-78-1
EPUB: 978-1-912478-76-7
PDF: 978-1-912478-77-4
AUDIO: 978-1-912478-79-8

Laurie Katz has asserted her right under the Copyright,
Design and Patents Act 1988 to be identified as the author of this work

Cover design and typeset by Fusion Graphic Design Ltd

Printed and bound in Great Britain by Clays Ltd, Elcograf S.p.A

Paper from responsible sources

www.triggerpublishing.com

*Thank you for purchasing this book.*
*You are making an incredible difference.*

Proceeds from all Trigger books go directly to
The Shaw Mind Foundation, a global charity that focuses
entirely on mental health. To find out more about
The Shaw Mind Foundation visit,
**www.shawmindfoundation.org**

## MISSION STATEMENT

*Our goal is to make help and support available for every*
*single person in society, from all walks of life.*
*We will never stop offering hope. These are our promises.*
Trigger and The Shaw Mind Foundation

Creating hope for children,
adults and families

## A NOTE FROM THE SERIES EDITOR

The Inspirational range from Trigger brings you genuine stories about our authors' experiences with mental health problems.

Some of the stories in our Inspirational range will move you to tears. Some will make you laugh. Some will make you feel angry, or surprised, or uplifted. Hopefully they will all change the way you see mental health problems.

These are stories we can all relate to and engage with. Stories of people experiencing mental health difficulties and finding their own ways to overcome them with dignity, humour, perseverance and spirit.

Laurie's brave and timely story doesn't just explore the consequences of being a victim of rape and sexual assault, but the wider ramifications in a victim's world. The trauma, disbelief, and the lack of support Laurie experienced are difficult to read about, and say so much about the attitudes of people and institutions towards victims of sexual assault. And yet, Laurie's story is ultimately and profoundly inspiring. Her reflections on her experiences range from very distressing to a more hopeful approach, and she shows us that inner strength, personal resolve, and the desire to live life on our own terms are stronger than anything.

This is our Inspirational range. These are our stories. We hope you enjoy them. And most of all, we hope that they will educate and inspire you. That's what this range is all about.

**Lauren Callaghan,**
*Co-founder and Lead Consultant Psychologist at Trigger*

*Dedicated to the memory of Andy (1989 – 2018).*
*Thank you for your belief in this book and in me.*
*I hope I do you proud.*

**Disclaimer:** Some names and identifying details have been changed to protect the privacy of individuals.

**Trigger Warning:** This book contains references to explicit sexual assault and rape.

# FOREWORD

Hi. You don't know me yet, but through reading this book you'll get to know me really well. My name is Laurie Koehler Katz. Sometimes I go by Laurie Koehler, because I get so tired of people mispronouncing my last name. It's pronounced "Kates". Yes, I know your mother-in-law / childhood best friend / barber pronounces it "Cats", but I come from a family of nonconformists. I grew up in Boston, feeding off the energy of the city, but always waiting for my time to leave and explore a new place. This new place would be Chicago. I came as a naive and eager freshman and left as a fractured and confused woman. On September 17, 2011, the third Saturday of college, I was raped. This is the story of everything connected and not connected to that night.

# CHAPTER 1

# *That Night*

I was drunk to the point that I could barely stand as I leaned against the wall of the apartment, wishing I was back at the dorm, in bed. People laughed and talked as I lowered my head and closed my eyes. It was the third Saturday of my freshman year at a large university in Chicago, and I went to an apartment off campus with some friends. I use the term "friends" loosely here. One was my friend Sarah from high school, and we were hanging out with a few guys who I had met that night.

Earlier in the evening, we had been drinking in a guy named Paul's dorm. I was on my first Four Loko of four and I felt like a badass. If you are not aware, Four Lokos are fruit – flavored malt liquor beverages that are popular with high school and college students. They contain about four shots worth of alcohol, and are commonly referred to as "blackout in a can."

As I drank my disgustingly sweet beverage, we heard a knock on the door and I watched everyone hide their drinks. No one said a word; they just calmly put their drinks out of sight. One guy even put his beer in a drawer. I frantically put my watermelon Four Loko behind my back and Paul opened the door. A Resident Assistant (RA) then told us to, "Keep the volume down." RAs are slightly older students who can live in the dorms for free if they watch out for, and supervise, their younger peers. This RA didn't even come into the room. The thrill of not getting caught was exciting. We were drinking in the dorm and no one could stop us. I used to wonder whether my life would be better if that RA had caught us drinking, and the rest of that night had never happened.

This was the pre-gaming phase of the night (drinking and socializing before actually going out). Afterwards, we went to a party that was marginally fun, in an apartment off campus. The host was beyond drunk and her friends seemed annoyed when so many freshmen showed up. After the party died down, the people I had pre-gamed with went to the playground of a local elementary school to play around and sober up.

I swung on one of the swings and this guy Steven, who was friends with Paul, started talking to me. This was exciting for about two minutes, until I realized he was just asking if I wanted to pay him to get me food. Apparently, he was asking everyone. When I told him that I didn't want any, he walked away.

It was getting colder and it was late, so Sarah, Paul, Steven, and I went to an apartment off campus to avoid getting in trouble for going back to our dorms drunk. Sarah and I had met two of the guys who lived in the apartment before, when they had helped us lug a vacuum from the dorm mailroom to our dorm. Remember that vacuum.

There was a policy stating that if you showed up to the dorm drunk, you could get in serious trouble and even be kicked out of the dorm. I had even heard of them calling ambulances for people who were not drunk enough to need an ambulance – that was probably meant to keep people from dying, but it made us afraid to go home, so we stayed out.

At the apartment, everyone found a seat in the living room while I went to the bathroom. Sarah and I had gotten ready for the night listening to M83's "Midnight City" on repeat and I had experimented with my make-up, wanting to look grown-up and less like myself. In the mirror my make-up was wrecked, and I did my best to fix what I could with some wet toilet paper.

When I came out there was nowhere to sit, so I crossed the room and leaned against the wall, struggling to stay awake. One of the guys who lived there asked me if I wanted to lie down. I followed him into his bedroom and promptly passed out. For the purposes of this book, I will call him "Noah." I could never write out his real name countless times or make myself read it. Actually, I'm going to change everyone's names because they are real people and anything else would be unfair. I will not include the name of my university or the names of things that might make them identifiable either, because what happened were the actions of a few people and do not reflect the university as a whole. (More importantly, I do not want to be sued).

While I was unconscious, my friends left the apartment to go smoke in a park. Noah woke me up and we started making out. When he took off my shirt I told him, "You can take my bra off if you want to." By the time my friends came back, he was finished. He went to greet them and as they got settled, I was just exiting his bedroom. I wanted to leave the apartment. I begged my friend Sarah, my best friend since ninth grade geometry class, to come with me. She wanted to stay, so I left the apartment alone and went back to my dorm.

I don't know how long I sat on my bed. One of my roommates came home. I cannot remember if she asked me if I was okay or if I just started talking. I told her my friends had left me passed out in a guy's bedroom. She had no response, but speaking to her snapped me out of it. I needed to do something. I spent the next three hours in the shower.

It took me months to fully remember that night. It came back to me in pieces.

Our conversation when I had been leaning on the wall outside his bedroom door. He loved Chicago and earlier that day, his grandfather had taken him grocery shopping. We had both gone to Montessori schools and he was new to the school too; he had just transferred. The smell of my perfume. The glass of orange juice on his bedside table. His amber eyes. The song

"The Way We Get By," which had been playing from his computer as I passed out. How he'd asked me if I was "comfy." How quickly things had changed and the realization that we were alone in the apartment. The dim lighting and how nauseous I was from the Four Lokos I'd had to drink. The physical pain that stayed with me for weeks.

What never left me though were those 10 words, "You can take my bra off if you want to." I'd never said those words before. I'd never had any intention of having sex with him. So then why had I told him he could take my bra off? What had I expected to happen? The guilt of those words stayed with me when I looked down at my body in the shower and saw the bite marks and bruises. In the months that followed, when I was too afraid to fall asleep until the sun came up and when I agonized over pursuing legal action, they were all I could hear. I felt dirty. I felt responsible.

# CHAPTER 2

# The Dean of Students

Here is how trauma affects the brain. The part of your brain responsible for executive functions more or less shuts down, and your brain doesn't waste energy on making new memories. All of your energy is put into surviving. When you're met with an experience that is terrifying, you either fight, run away, or (what happened to me) freeze. Freezing is your body's last resort when your brain believes that you are going to die. If you are frozen you cannot protect yourself, but your brain is then able to minimize the fear and pain. It's like playing dead. If you don't move, maybe you'll be hurt less. I actually do not think saying fight, flight, *or* freeze is really accurate. When I realized we were alone in the apartment I tried to leave (flight), when he started to get forceful I tried to push him away (fight), and when that didn't work, I froze.

I struggled with my memories and feelings about that night. I knew that what happened hadn't been right, but did that make it rape? People got grabbed in dark alleys and raped at gunpoint. They didn't pass out in a stranger's bed and wake up to them kissing and undressing them.

After that night, I began to deteriorate rapidly. I was conflicted about what had happened, but I was certain about how terrified and ashamed I felt. In those first weeks, the only time I was out of the dorm was for class. I had begun to struggle with severe depression and anxiety.

After two weeks, and in a moment of desperation, I knocked on my RA's door and told her what had happened. Or I implied it. I couldn't bring myself to say anything specific.

"A couple weeks ago, I went to an apartment and I was drunk and I passed out and my friends left me and something happened."

The only thing that sticks out in my memory that my RA said was, "If this happened a couple weeks ago, why is it bothering you now?"

Did this mean I should have been over it? Or had what happened not been bad enough, if it took me two weeks to tell anyone?

The next day a woman from housing services called me. I'm assuming my RA was following some sort of protocol by telling this woman.

"I heard that you think something might have happened a few weeks ago."

"Um, yeah," I replied, humiliated.

"What do you want to do?"

"I think I want to go to the police." I was struggling with whether that was what I wanted to do. I had washed away evidence, but I was still bruised and that had to count for something.

"You think you want to go to the police? Or you want to go to the police?"

"I want to go to the police."

"So that would mean calling the police, and if you do that they would have to come all the way to campus and you don't want to waste their time, right?"

Of course I didn't want to waste their time. Clearly, what he did to me didn't matter enough to get the police involved, and I felt ridiculous for suggesting it.

"Your best option is to let the university handle it."

So, the woman persuaded me that the best thing to do would be to have a judicial case through my university's hearing committee. This meant meeting with the Dean of Students at my school and having to tell more people about what happened. I was afraid of what this case would mean, but I felt I needed to do something.

I looked up who the Dean of Students was and was a little apprehensive that it turned out to be a guy. But I decided this was something I needed to do. I emailed the Dean of Students to set up a meeting and, a few days later, I met with him to get some information on what a case would look like. I sat in his office on the second floor of the Student Center (the building on campus that houses the dining hall and administrative offices) and the large windows made me feel less trapped during our meeting. The Dean was in his mid- to late-thirties and had a calming way about him.

I sat facing his desk and could barely bring myself to look at him. I was so humiliated. I had a piece of paper in my hands from one of my classes that I kept folding into smaller and smaller pieces.

"What would a case look like if a student was assaulted?" I asked him. Even just saying "assaulted" was almost too much for me at this time and it felt better to ask for some hypothetical student and not myself.

"If a student was assaulted," he told me, "the first thing this student would need to do would be to write an account of what happened."

He explained that for the case, I would need to write up an account of that night and so would Noah. Then, based on that, Noah would either be found responsible or not – the university's terminology for guilty or not guilty. There would be a hearing and we both would be there, so I would have to face Noah. The Dean assured me that we would be separated by a screen, and as we all know, screens are soundproof. This made me incredibly anxious, but if found "responsible" Noah could have been suspended or expelled, so I decided it was worth it. I was too humiliated to ask anyone who had been there that night to testify (not that I was told that this was even an option), so I just went about typing up my account. But it wasn't that easy.

I tried to write out the narrative, but I was missing so many pieces. I could remember flashes of me just lying there. Why hadn't I fought harder? I could remember saying, "You can take my bra off if you want to," but that had been when he had seemed normal and I had never wanted anything more. So it was still rape, right? I don't know for certain what I wrote in my account because I have since deleted the file from my computer, not wanting to ever look at it again after the whole mess was over. But I wrote out what had happened as best I could.

The Dean had to be impartial I guess, but he seemed to genuinely believe me (when I finally admitted that the "student" I was referring to was me). When meeting with him I felt that I was being taken seriously and justice would happen. He was incredibly kind and acted like he cared. He didn't just talk to me about the case. He asked questions about how I was doing and what I was majoring in. His kindness made me feel that I was making the right decisions.

The case had many starts and stops. Some were my fault. I was afraid and confused. Some were just due to timing, such as a vacation (by the time the hearing was going to start, my university was starting a six-week break). Getting all of the players together wasn't easy either. During the time before and after the break, I was missing class and not turning in assignments. At the time, not coming back after vacation never occurred to me as an option. I was a college freshman and going back to school after vacation was what college freshmen did. The time away did make me feel more committed to the case and let me recharge a bit for what was to come.

At school, leaving my dorm was a terrifying event and I started having panic attacks. In January, the Dean said he would email my professors to let them know I had an excuse for my missing assignments and for missing class. When I went to speak with my rhetoric professor about some missing assignments, I brought up the email from the Dean.

"What email? You have until tomorrow to turn in all of your papers, or you will fail the class."

My professor told me to come to his office early the next morning to turn in my work and discuss my place in the class. I pulled an all-nighter, throwing every assignment together as best I could. I remember that one of the assignments was to create an ad for anything you wanted. I made an advertisement for Verizon that featured the main cast of *Pretty Little Liars* staring at their phones. It's a famous shot from the TV show. My tagline was, "Say goodbye to pretty little late fees." I thought that was clever.

I emailed the Dean to ask if he had emailed my professors as he said he would. He never responded. I made a lot of excuses for the Dean, thinking that he had my best interests at heart and that his non-response didn't mean he wasn't doing anything.

The next morning, half asleep, I walked to my professor's office to turn in my assignments. Sitting in front of his desk, I felt like a child in the principal's office. I had never had to meet with a teacher or a professor for anything that wasn't positive. There I was on the verge of failing his class and I felt like a failure. As I sat, I looked around his small, windowless office and at the pictures on his walls. It was too overwhelming to look at him and face how much control I had lost over my life and the failures this was creating. I wondered about one of the pictures of him that kind of looked like an ad, and I wondered if he had really been in an ad. This was my train of thought as he berated me for missing class. No, not berated. He wasn't interested in why I had missed class and I don't think he was terribly interested in whether I would miss any more. He just told me, "If you miss one more class, you will automatically fail." It was then that I realized missing class and not doing my work would hurt me, and that excuses don't mean much in college.

I didn't miss any more classes. Most nights I lay in bed terrified, waiting for the sun to come up. When my panic became overwhelming and I needed to get out of the dark, I would walk around the dorm or sit in the bright laundry room, sometimes up to between 10 and 15 times a night. My roommates had no idea what I was going through and they probably found me crazy and annoying. I sometimes watched Netflix, but the brightness bothered my roommates as they tried to sleep, and there was no reason for all of us to suffer. I tried melatonin and Tylenol PM, but nothing helped. I usually felt safe to fall asleep around eight in the morning, and with my class schedule my alarm went off at 10:00.

Time chugged on and finally the case was done, but it wasn't like I had been told it would be. I never had to face Noah. I never gave any testimony. I never went to a hearing. I just got an email that he had been found responsible and would be suspended for two terms. One of those terms would be in the summer when barely anyone took classes, so it really boiled down to a ten-week suspension. I was still relieved that I was getting some sort of justice; not the expulsion I had wanted, but something. But I was also confused about how they had had a hearing without me there. Still, I felt validated. What happened had mattered enough for him to at least be suspended. The Dean emailed to say this was effective immediately and to let him know if I saw Noah on campus, as he would be banned from the premises for the entirety of his suspension.

I wanted to jump up and down. My relief could not be contained. I was free for the time being and that was something. I ignored how weird the case had been and focused on this gift of time and justice. That night, I walked to the Student Center for dinner and I wasn't afraid. I didn't have to walk quickly with my head down; I could walk proudly. This was my campus for the next few months and I would enjoy it.

But when I got to the Student Center, there was Noah eating his dinner like nothing was wrong. He was with his group of friends and they were talking and laughing. Noah had dark hair and was on the shorter side, but fit. I would have known him anywhere.

When I saw Noah, I started to shake. The sounds of people eating and talking became muffled. It felt like I was underwater – water that was unbearably hot. My heart was beating faster than was safe and I felt like I needed to throw up. I somehow made it to the bathroom and sat on the cool floor while trying to breathe. I was shaking too much and the tears were coming. I felt like I was going to pass out and I laid down on the floor. Feeling the cool tile on my face, I started to calm down. Writing this now, I'm a bit disturbed that I touched my face to the floor of a public bathroom. Gross. After I had calmed down enough I wanted to leave, but I was afraid I would run into Noah if I left the bathroom. So, I waited and waited some more. When I felt enough time had passed, I ran back shakily to the dorm. I emailed the Dean to let him know I had seen Noah at the Student Center. He never responded.

A week later, I got an email telling me that Noah had appealed the decision, was found "not responsible" this time, and was back at school. So that was that. He missed one week of school and that was his punishment. The case was over and the result was nothing. What I believed was confirmed. What he had done to me didn't matter enough to warrant even a short suspension. It didn't matter at all.

He had appealed his case to the Vice President of Student Affairs, a woman I would soon have the misfortune of knowing. I had been relieved that I hadn't had to see Noah or testify at the hearing, but maybe if I had been given the chance, things would have ended differently. After the sham of my case, I decided I needed to try to put what had happened behind me and move on.

And I did. For a few months I was somewhat okay. This would change.

# CHAPTER 3

## Court

When Noah started following and harassing me to the point that I had to go to court and get an Emergency Order of Protection (basically a restraining order), I still continued to feel responsible for all that had happened. He just seemed to be wherever I was, even off campus when I went to my internship. Usually he just stood across the street from wherever I was and watched me. I mostly saw him standing in the parking lot across the street from my dorm.

Things started slowly and then escalated. He started yelling at me about "how much fun our night together had been." And how "it was our secret." He cornered me outside one of my classes and told me that his dad had a gun and he had access to it. I wasn't sure if he was lying, but this scared me.

In February of my freshman year, I went to the Cook County Court House in Chicago for a day filled with ridicule and humiliation. In the courtroom, I had to explain the harassment to the judge and how I knew Noah. The room was filled with law students and other people waiting to go before the judge, and they watched the events unfold like a TV show. I had spent hours at the courthouse being shuffled around and made to fill out sheet after sheet of paperwork. Going to court isn't like how they show it in the movies.

Most of my time that day was spent in a large room, with hundreds of other people who were waiting to get called up to fill out more paperwork. When you got called up, you were sent to a big round table where one woman helped everyone get seated (about 10 people at a time) and fill out the papers that they needed. There was no privacy. I don't know how many times that day I had to say, "I was sexually assaulted, and the guy is now following and harassing me," to a room full of strangers.

I made a mistake on one of papers and wrote my actual home address in Massachusetts. I was exhausted and had never thought of the dorm as where I really lived.

"You're getting an Order of Protection in Chicago, but you live in Massachusetts?" the woman helping everyone with the paperwork asked me.

"Oh, that was a mistake. I live in a dorm in Chicago."

A woman seated next to me started laughing. "You wrote the wrong address on a form for court?"

I didn't respond to her. I knew if I tried to speak, I would cry. No one was given new forms if they made a mistake. I was handed white-out and I set about fixing the form.

When it was my turn to go into the courtroom to go before the judge, I was relieved when I saw that the judge was a woman. Once in the courtroom, I still had to wait about 10 more minutes and I sat in one of the courtroom pews in the back of the room. The courtroom was small and windowless; I felt overheated and trapped as I waited. I listened to a man go before the judge for his own Order of Protection, and though I would not wish this on anyone, it made me feel better to see the process. I listened to his story and others listened to mine. No privacy.

When they called "Laurie Cats", I got up from my pew and walked up the aisle to stand in front of the judge. I had taken a bootcamp workout class the day before and my body was ridiculously sore. Just sitting in the pew and having to stand up made my muscles groan. Maybe that's not terribly important to what happened in the courtroom, but it's what I remember.

I walked up the aisle to stand before the judge. Looking up at her sitting on the raised bench, I felt impossibly small.

"State your full name and date of birth," the court clerk said.

"Laurie Koehler Katz. May 28, 1993."

He then told me to raise my right hand and said, "Do you solemnly swear to tell the truth, the whole truth and nothing but the truth, so help you God?"

I just stood there, staring at him. I had seen enough TV shows and movies to know how to respond, but that part of my brain was not working in that moment. He looked annoyed and stared back at me.

"You have to respond," he said.

I took a shaky breath. "Yes, um, um, I do." And so, the hearing began.

When the judge asked me how I knew Noah, I repeated my mantra of the day. "I was sexually assaulted, and the guy is now following and harassing me."

"If he raped you, why didn't you go to the police?" she asked me.

I still cannot be completely sure how to answer this. I had been alone in a new city, in shock and confused about what had happened. I was terrified and just wanted to take a shower and leave the night behind. I was so many things that night that it wouldn't occur to me to go to the police for another two weeks, and then I would be told not to.

"I didn't have any evidence," was the only response I deemed worthy to tell the judge.

"Did he ejaculate?"

"Yes."

"Then you had evidence."

There it was. I wasn't the "perfect" victim. I didn't tell anyone for two weeks, but I did what I thought was right that night to take care of myself and keep myself safe.

As I looked up at the judge, the muscles in my face started to tighten and my eyes watered. I bit my cheek to stop myself from crying and I wouldn't let myself take a breath. Breathing meant the tears would come. I didn't know how to respond to her statement and I felt worthless.

I got the Order of Protection and it lasted for a whole 30 days. I was supposed to go back to try to renew it, but I was too afraid to face Noah and I would have to face him alone. It was explained to me, by the woman who helped me fill out the paperwork, that at the hearing in 30 days Noah and I would each tell our side of the story. Then the judge and Noah could interrogate me about it while I took the stand. That terrified me. Going back would also mean missing my rhetoric class and that would mean failing. The 30 days ran out, but I think it scared him into stopping, because he didn't harass me anymore. I didn't feel any safer during those 30 days; I felt like I had a target on my back. About a week after I missed the hearing, I got a postcard in my dorm mailbox to tell me that the case had been dropped.

There was one nice person in that courtroom. There was a man who took the signed Order of Protection from the judge, to file it or something. I don't know what his title was, but he treated me like a person. He must have read my address on my paperwork because he said, "Oh, you must go to [insert name of my school here]." He made a little more small talk with me and his kindness surprised me. No one wants to go to court; it's just as easy to be kind as to be cruel.

I wish our court system was different and that all judges were compassionate. I know there have to be some kind judges out there, but I wasn't so lucky that day. And why should someone who fears for their life have to be interrogated by the perpetrator to get protection? In the end it was a good thing that I got the Emergency Order of Protection, even if it was temporary. Noah ended up transferring and moving away after my freshman year.

# CHAPTER 4

## The Email

It was Tuesday, May 29, 2012. I know this because I remember that the class I almost missed that night was about integrating arts into curriculum, and this met on Tuesday nights. I also know this because the day before had been my 19th birthday, a day of seeing cute aquarium animals at The Shedd and eating sushi (I know, horrible) and cupcakes. I had felt genuinely happy for the first time in months.

That Tuesday morning, I woke up with the feeling that something bad was going to happen. I'd had a nightmare and the sick feeling of it permeated through my day. I went to the gym after class, as I did almost every day. After I ran my obligatory miles, I decided it was time to leave. I left the gym and started my walk back to the dorm; it was warm out and I felt an adrenaline high. As I got closer to my dorm, I saw that the street was blocked off. I could see police officers and the sky was full of black clouds of smoke Clearly there was a fire somewhere nearby. Could it be the dorm?

*19th birthday – with no idea of what was to come.*

My first thought was, *but all my things are in there!* I couldn't be bothered to be worried about my roommates or the hundreds of students in the dorm. I speed walked to my block and a police officer told me that I could only enter the block if I lived in the dorm or was going to the post office. Relief swept through me. That meant it wasn't the dorm.

"I live in the dorm. What's going on?"

"Ron's Furniture is on fire," she replied.

This was the first time I had even heard that there was a furniture store near my dorm. I walked the final block and could see a fire truck, but not the actual fire. The quietness of the whole operation was striking. There were no shouting or sirens, just firemen methodically doing what they do every day.

I entered my dorm and started the trudge up the four flights of stairs. I felt a sense of relief, which built with each flight I conquered. The fire must have been the bad thing that was going to happen. The relief came in knowing what the bad thing was and that it was terrible, but nothing to do with me. I took a shower and got dressed for class. From my dorm room's window I could see the firemen with their hoses, on the roof of the building next door. In theory this probably sounds exciting, but after a few moments it was actually pretty boring. I didn't have any pressing work to do and I had about an hour to fill before class.

Both of my roommates were in the room, which rarely happened. I was feeling self-conscious and claustrophobic. They were fine, but we were never friends. I had requested a non-smoking roommate, so of course I got two smokers. The only thing we all had in common was our favorite cereal, Honey Bunches of Oats. Each of my roommates commented on the fire and then we continued to pretend we were all alone in the room. I decided to check my email. This being a few years before I would get an iPhone, checking my email was a daily production that could only be completed on my laptop.

The email I found in my inbox would haunt me for the next

four years-maybe even for the rest of my life. It was from the Vice President of Student Affairs at my school. It was a formal email. Clinical and impersonal. I wish that I had saved it, but my mortification caused me to delete most emails from that time. The email was to inform me that a judicial case was being started against me for providing false information in a judicial case. False information? That could only mean that I was being accused of making the whole thing up, that I had been pretending to be raped. I immediately emailed the woman back and asked what was going on. I got an automated response from her saying that she would be at a retreat for the rest of the week. I emailed the Dean of Students and begged him to let me know what was happening. He never responded to that email.

I felt my stomach churning, like I needed to throw up. And I needed to cry. I stood up from my desk, left my room, and walked around the corner to the laundry room in the dorm. The laundry room had become my sanctuary for private moments and phone calls. It was usually empty, save for the weekends, and it was more or less soundproof. I entered the room and the fluorescent light brightly illuminated the space as it always did. A lone washer chugged away, and I found my safe space on the side of the machines, where a sink was hidden. If anyone opened the door, the room would look empty. I sat on the floor and started crying.

I did not think it was possible to cry as hard as I did that day on the floor of the laundry room. I didn't cry like that after being raped and I haven't cried that hard since. I think every person might be allotted one "hardest cry of your life", and this was mine.

As I cried I thought to myself, *I can either kill myself or go to class.* Those two options continued playing in my mind. *Kill yourself or go to class. Kill yourself or go to class. Kill yourself or go to class.* I tried to breathe, but I had forgotten how. *Kill yourself or go to class.* I didn't feel that my life had any value. I didn't know what was going on and I was scared and confused. I felt so stupid for feeling somewhat okay and thinking it was all over. My birthday had been perfect and that only added to how ridiculous I felt. How could I have allowed myself to have fun? Was this my punishment?

If I missed class it would hurt my grade. I continued crying and tried to think of ways to commit suicide that would be the most effective, with the least amount of pain. I couldn't decide if I wanted to commit suicide, and I wasn't sure if I truly wanted to die, but deciding on a plan for how I would do it made everything feel more manageable. I didn't have to be here. It was my choice and if I wanted to die, I could. If I was dead, no one could hurt me, and school wouldn't matter. I decided that I would go to class and I could decide if I wanted to kill myself later.

After a few days of panic, the woman got back to my email and scheduled a time to call me to discuss the case and schedule the hearing. For this phone call I sat in my dorm room closet, beyond caring if my roommates heard.

I sat on the floor with my back against the wall of my closet, remembering how my mom had helped me unpack my things when I had moved in.

The Vice President of Student Affairs was chipper on the phone and her voice sounded like she was sporting a smirk.

"Why is this happening now?" I asked her.

"At the end of every school year, we review all of the cases that are brought to the Dean of Students, and there were some inconsistencies in yours."

This changed everything. From the wording of the email and my understanding of the way these cases came to be, I had assumed that Noah had started a case against me. Clearly this wasn't the case. The university had decided to start a case against me.

"Is the student I had the other case with not involved in this case?" I couldn't bring myself to say his name.

"No, this is through the university. Noah is not a part of this case."

Noah. Just hearing his name made me want to cry.

"It's been months since my case. I still don't understand. Why is the school coming after me now?"

She cheerily informed me, "No one is "coming after you". We just have to review your case. It was dragged out for quite a while and this has been extremely emotional for Noah and his family."

"Extremely emotional for Noah and his family." I harbored so much guilt surrounding that night and I felt myself questioning my own understanding of what had happened and my right to my feelings. If it was emotional for Noah, could it be emotional for me?

As I spoke to this woman, she explained that Noah had apparently told her about the Emergency Order of Protection and how I had not renewed it, and this made me look less reliable. I felt so stupid for not going back to court, but it confused me why any of that should have any bearing on the case that I had with the school.

The hearing was set for the following Monday, the first day of final exams. I sat in my closet and cried, feeling so angry with myself for the mess I had gotten myself into.

In the lead up to that meeting, I couldn't sleep and eating was out of the question. I stayed up late, trying to feel safe in the dark. I tried to study, but my mind kept going over every detail of that night. I reread my statement to the Dean of Students over and over, trying to find what I had said to incriminate myself.

# CHAPTER 5

## The Hearing

After almost a week since receiving the email, it was finally Monday and time for the hearing. The only time the Vice President of Student Affairs was free was first thing in the morning, so after a night of waiting for the sun to come up so I could feel safe again, I made my way to her office.

My eyes hurt and my head was throbbing from the lack of sleep. My vision felt almost blurry and I kept rubbing my eyes. Once I got to her office, I knew I had to get it together. I felt an empty ache in my stomach, a pleasing reminder that I hadn't eaten. The choice to not eat made me feel like I had something I could control, and the emptiness was comforting. According to the National Eating Disorders Association (NEDA), 30–65% of people who struggle with eating disorders have experienced some sort of sexual trauma. For me, not eating and obsessively working out gave me control over the body that had been wrecked and ruined. Before receiving the email about the hearing against me, I had been doing better overall and felt moments of true happiness, but I was still suffering. I had recently begun attempting to have a better relationship with food – look out for the time I eat Sun Chips in a later chapter – but leading up to the hearing, not eating and working out harder and longer gave me a distinct focus and false sense of control.

For the hearing, I was wearing the purple t-shirt from The Gap that I had worn the previous spring when my dad and I had visited the school. I had chosen it because it was modest and I was afraid to paint a bad impression of myself. I also wore jeans, a decision that I regretted as I sat in the waiting room. Do innocent girls wear jeans? Couldn't I have worn my black pants that I had bought for internships?

I checked in with the Vice President of Student Affairs' secretary and proceeded to sit in the waiting room for close to an hour. Every minute that passed I wanted to leave, but that would only make me look guiltier. Had I come at the wrong time? No. I was sure of it. My anxiety about the meeting was reaching a critical point and I was tearing up. "Please don't cry," I told myself. I needed to get through this meeting and crying would make that impossible. I replayed that night and the aftermath in my head, searching for what I had done to end up here.

My only comfort was my option of suicide. When I had decided I couldn't take it any longer, the woman emerged from her office. I had assumed that she was running late and was on her way from a different location. No, she had been in her office the whole time, knowing that I was there, waiting. She was middle aged with short blonde hair. Her physique was short and large. I'm not saying that to be mean or catty; that's just how she looked.

I stood up and shook her hand, wondering about how normal this interaction must have looked to her receptionist. We walked to a conference room in the office suite and I took a seat. The lighting was dim and the room was windowless. I felt trapped. The first thing she said to me was, "You look different to what I was expecting." I guess the jeans hadn't come off too bad.

The next hour or so was confusing and humiliating. She barked questions at me that spun me in circles and left me questioning whether I even knew anything about what had happened that night and the months afterward. I felt tricked and I found myself contradicting myself. She wanted me to read Noah's account and got angry when I refused. There it sat on the table in a manila folder mocking me for the entirety of the meeting.

"Hmmm," she said as she leaned back in her chair, crossing her arms and smiling at me. "So, you willingly went into his bedroom. Is there anything you want to share with me now?"

There was so much I wanted to say, but I was too afraid that I would incriminate myself further. I was facing possible suspension or expulsion.

"Well, I'm not going to lie, this is not looking good for you. You dragged this case out for months." She waited for a response that I could not give. "Noah was suspended for two terms and then his suspension was lifted after a week. Would you like to know why that was?"

I thought back to the last time I had been able to look down in the shower. It hadn't been the bruises and bite marks. It had been the blood. Reminding me of all I had lost.

"You claim that he started harassing you, but that's highly unusual. Men don't rape first and then start harassing their victim. It happens the other way around."

I tried to think if that made sense.

"And you didn't go to the police? If he did the things you wrote about, I find it hard to believe you wouldn't go to the police right away or soon after."

*But I was told not to. I thought I was doing the right thing. The school told me not to.*

She stared at me and I opened my mouth, but no words came out.

"We might have to put a letter in your file so that if something like this ever happens again, we'll know it's "Liar Laurie.""

Liar Laurie. Why had I ever told anyone what had happened?

She said they would have five days to decide if I was "responsible", and what that would mean for me.

That night, I had my final for one of my education classes. I sat at my desk in the classroom and tried to remember the material. Around me my classmates frantically answered the multiple-choice questions and wrote their essays, but it just felt pointless. I hadn't been able to study with everything going on. The exam and school itself had lost their importance. I was going to kill myself, so I left half of the exam paper blank.

That night, thoughts of my suicide tormented me. I got close, but I couldn't give in to them, because I had a glimmer of hope that the case would be okay. The worst part, I told myself, was over. And they had to see that they were wrong. Didn't they?

The week continued on in this way and I checked my email every day, at every chance I got. My exams continued and I did the best I could. I was waiting for the decision of my hearing, still hoping that they would realize they were wrong about me. I even believed that the Dean of Students would respond to my email and that he would help me. I had my suicide planned, but I just needed to know what the outcome of my case was.

I would see the Vice President of Student Affairs one more time. It was a couple of days before I went home for the summer, my freshman year. I went to return my books to a van by the Student Center, which gave marginally better buy-back prices than the school bookstore. She was leaving the Student Center and she glanced over at me and kept walking. I was relieved that I was wearing another t-shirt with a high neck.

Finally, it was Friday and I could go home to Boston. The second I got home I checked my email. Another formal email greeted me to say I had been found "responsible" for providing false information in a judicial case. A letter saying this would be put in my file. I guess I was grateful that I wasn't suspended or expelled.

It's not surprising that I was found responsible. My university got to be the plaintiff, judge, and jury. Still, the outcome gutted me. It was one thing that Noah was found not "responsible" (I wish I could just use the world "guilty"), it was another for the outcome to be this, whatever this was.

"Liar Laurie."

If he did anything else to me, I would be a marked liar and no one would believe me. If anything happened to me no one would believe me. I felt vulnerable and scared, but more than anything I felt defeated. I had tried to help myself, to get some sort of justice for myself, and somehow he had become the victim. It was devastating.

I promised myself then that when I was strong enough I would appeal the decision and have that letter removed from my file, but I was still so confused.

"You can take my bra off if you want to." The weight of those 10 words made me question if I had even been raped. The letter in my file from the university deepened my feelings of guilt and shame. I felt like a criminal. Did he really believe he hadn't raped me? In those 10 words had I given consent? So then he hadn't raped me, and I had created all these problems for myself.

No. I had struggled. He had been completely sober and I had been drunk for one of the first times in my life. But, had I actually said no? Or stop? I couldn't remember, and not remembering made me assume the worst of myself – or what I believed to be the worst of myself. He had used force, but with the burden of those words I ignored all these things and took the blame.

# CHAPTER 6

## Music Festival

Every year at the end of spring term, there was a music festival at my school. This was a time when hundreds of students gathered in the quad for an outdoor concert before finals, fueled by shots and Molly. The concert started in the late afternoon when it was still light out, and went on late into the night, with an afterparty in the school gym.

A pretty popular rapper headlined my freshman year festival. It was the beginning of June, three days after I received the email about the case against me from the Vice President of Student Affairs and three days before I would have my hearing, at which I would be dubbed Liar Laurie.

My friend Sarah and I had taken shots of sweet tea vodka and I was nauseous. We had pre-gamed a bit at the dorm and then some more at our friend Ryan's apartment. He didn't go to our school, so he couldn't go to the festival, but he knew how to get things that would make the night more fun. The music festival was an excuse to get out of my head and not care about the future.

Sarah and I entered the quad together and met up with our friend Aurora. As the night wore on I lost them in the crowd, but I couldn't let myself care. I was trashed.

I ran into a guy, Henry, from my statistics class. He was drinking out of a red Gatorade bottle and, feeling dehydrated, I asked if I could have some. It wasn't Gatorade. I couldn't figure out how he got a Gatorade bottle into the quad since they checked your bags when you came in. That night, I felt so ashamed of what was happening and I had lost control of my life once again. I didn't care what happened to me.

We ended up back at his apartment and going to his bedroom. I thought I could make myself be with him. It would mean that what had happened didn't matter, because sex didn't matter. But when it came to it I started to cry on his bed, as a program about cheese played silently on PBS in the background. After I freaked out, he got me a taxi home. Henry was a decent, normal person, who understood that going to someone's apartment and even being in bed with them is not consent.

My sophomore year, the festival was once again at the end of spring term. It was there that I saw the Dean of Students for the last time. To get into the festival you needed to wait in line to have your student ID and ticket scanned and, of course, your bag checked. You also needed to appear sober for the moments that this would take. And there the Dean was. Just standing there. He wasn't checking tickets or IDs or even minding the line. He was just there.

Earlier that afternoon, I had learned that I was banned from 1453. What's 1453, you say? 1453 is what we like to call 1453 West Faber. That's its address and its name. It's a building right off my school's campus and a "cool" place for students to live. It still has a front desk that people need to sign in to, but it's not a dorm, so it's the place to be. In my freshman year, 1453 had seemed a mystical place where there was an abundance of parties every night, if you could just get in the building. On the second weekend of school, one of my roommate's friends had said that she knew someone who knew a guy that lived there, and we could use his name to get into the building and find a party. So I had gotten glammed up, feeling so much excitement for the evening. We walked to 1453 and eagerly signed in with our school IDs. When we made it to my roommate's friend's friend's friend's room, we asked him where the party was.

"Party? I have no idea. I don't know of anything going on tonight."

So maybe 1453 wasn't the party haven we had built it up to be.

On September 17th of my freshman year, imagine my excitement to go to an apartment in 1453, after we left the playground. I knew all of the hype couldn't be wrong!

We all know how that story ends.

I would end up going to 1453 two or three more times my freshman year. I wanted to prove that I was fine and going there didn't bother me. One of those times I saw Tony, one of Noah's roommates, in the elevator, and that was too close a call. Sophomore year, my friend Polly lived in 1453. Polly and I met freshman year in the Student Center and she became my best friend in college. I never told her about what happened, and as I write this only a handful of people know.

After months of making excuses and only hanging out together at my apartment, I finally caved and went back to 1453. I ended up going to Polly's apartment two or three times. At the end of May, Polly and I had just come from a day of shopping and were going to her apartment to pre-game for the festival. I went to sign in like I would any other time, only this time the front desk man said, "I'm sorry your ID is coming up with a ban. I can't let you in."

We thought he was joking.

"No, I'm serious. You are banned. I cannot let you enter the building." He fetched a thick binder from behind his desk with the names of all of the people who were banned from the building and why.

He found my name and read, "It looks like an incident with a Noah Silverman."

But how could that be? I had been in Polly's apartment a week before, and after my freshman year Noah had moved away. The man said I could call the building manager for more information, but I was too humiliated. The entryway had filled with students trying to get in, and Polly wanted to know what was going on. I'll never know why that ban happened and why then, but it's just as well. It wasn't good for me to be in that space.

I had told myself that I wouldn't drink too much that night. I was coming off a year of partying and I didn't want to test my luck. The news of my ban changed everything.

By the time I saw the Dean, I was a bit out of my head. I wanted to say something to him or scream at him or something. I don't think he noticed me or really any of the students in particular. Maybe he was there for show? Or just to see what the festival was all about?

*How could you let them do that to me? Why didn't you respond to my email? Do you think I'm a liar? Why did you pretend to care?* I didn't say any of those things. I didn't say anything. I was drunk and had broken my seal, so I spent most of the night in line for the Porta Potty.

A popular trap music DJ was playing the festival that year. This was before he was big and I have to say, seeing a guy with his MacBook standing up on a stage in broad daylight is as exciting as it sounds. No shade to the DJ; I love to listen to his music while running, but this was not an amazing concert. In line for the Porta Potty, I shouted at anyone who would listen that the Dean of Students was there.

"The Dean's right over there!" I yelled. "Why do you think he's here?"

"Maybe he wants to see his students," a random girl replied.

"The Dean doesn't give a shit about his students," I near screamed, hoping he heard me.

Remember, trap music. Hundreds of students shouting and singing along. Boy did I give that Dean what was coming to him!

My junior year, the festival was headlined by one of my favorite rappers, who also happens to be one of my favorite comedians and has starred in one of my favorite shows. He was pretty awesome live. Is there anything this guy can't do? An indie rock band opened the show and it made me miss my best friend Sarah so much it hurt. We had loved them together in high school. More on Sarah later.

Splitting a bottle of Tequila with Polly added to the fun and misery of that night. I had more or less sworn off alcohol, but this was the music festival! We'd realized by this point that it was pretty easy to sneak booze into the quad, i.e. tampon shots. If the Dean was there, I was ready to let him have it!

I didn't see the Dean, but I did spend a good part of the night throwing up.

My senior year, the festival was amazing. By this point things had changed in my life.

# CHAPTER 7

# Meaning Well

You might be wondering where my parents were through all of this, so let me tell you. In February of my freshman year, you already know that things were not going too well. The case had been put on hold for winter break, and trying to get the case to start up again was not easy. It was like starting from square one. I was still unsure of what I wanted and being home for six weeks made me question if doing a case was worth it. When Noah had started harassing and following me, I decided I needed to go through with the hearing. I needed him off campus so I could feel safe and try to get my life back to normal, and I wanted him held accountable for what he did to me. I met with the Dean to discuss the case and to get things going again. I also told him about the harassment.

The Dean contacted me a few days later and asked me to come and meet with him. When I got to his office he told me, "I'm going to call your parents and let them know what happened." I was shocked and sickened by this. He had tricked me into coming to his office. I felt the room closing in on me and my heart started pumping loudly in my ears. I felt like I was going to pass out. When this happens to me, something that usually helps is drinking water. I didn't have any water, but I had a Diet Pepsi from the Student Center (why can places never carry Coke?). I leaned over, took my Diet Pepsi from my backpack, and took a giant swig of it, just trying to ground myself.

The Dean picked up the phone and asked me for my parents' number. "If you don't tell me, I can just look it up," he told me. I gulped down my swig of soda and stared at the bottle. I told him the number and looked up to watch him type it out on the black phone on his desk.

As the reality of what was happening began to sink in, I knew I had to get out of there. The large windows in his office were no longer enough to keep me from feeling trapped. I got up and walked out of his office. By the time I got to the stairs I was running, and soon I was out the door of the Student Center. Immediately a blast of February Chicago air hit me and I realized that I was screwed. In my haste to leave I had left my coat and backpack (and Diet Pepsi) in the Dean's office. The only way to get in to my dorm was with your school ID or if someone who lived there signed you in, but you still needed an ID for that. Crap. How was I going to get back into my dorm? My phone, my wallet, everything was upstairs by his desk. I was freezing and panicking. And if I went to the dorm, what would happen? Would the Dean send someone to find me? Crap. The longer I was outside, the colder I got. As I sat on a bench outside the Student Center, I saw Polly. She was coming to the Student Center to talk to someone in the Dean's suite about getting a discount on her car insurance. She asked if I wanted to go with her. To the Dean's suite. The place I had just run out of. Crap. I had no coat, no money, no student ID, and no options, so I went back.

We entered the door I had just run out of and walked up the backstairs.

"Where's your coat?" Polly asked me.

"I left it somewhere."

"Aren't you cold?"

"Not really." *Yes Polly, I'm freezing.*

We entered the Dean's suite and Polly started talking to someone at the front desk. I kept walking, entering the Dean's office without signing in. I just walked in. Polly later asked me what had happened, because I had just "disappeared."

When I entered his office, the Dean didn't look surprised. He'd been waiting for me. I sat down and saw my things just as I had left them.

"So, your dad is flying out tomorrow to come see you."

"What if I don't let him into my dorm?"

"I'm going to contact your dorm to make sure he's allowed in."

Interesting how the Dean could contact my dorm to force something on me, but couldn't be bothered to contact my professors to help me.

The Dean didn't apologize or explain why he did it. I didn't know at the time that informing my parents without my consent was actually illegal. Can you say Family Educational Rights and Privacy Act (FERPA) violation? It's hard to say if he wanted to get my parents freaked out so I would drop out or if he just couldn't (wouldn't) handle the situation.

A day later, my dad met me at my dorm and I signed him in. We had a somewhat normal dinner, and the next morning he forced me to go to court for the Protection Order. There was no discussion about what my options were or about what would happen when I got to court. I was never asked if I wanted to do this – I was told I had to. At court, I refused to speak to my dad and kept him away from me. I don't think my dad knew how to help me and taking over was all he knew.

I hope I don't sound like a brat. I know my parents wanted to help me and they didn't know how. I didn't tell them about what had happened because I was confused and embarrassed. Not telling your parents is incredibly common for people who have been raped. I couldn't handle what I was going through and this was just too much for me.

I had been violated in a horrific manner and I needed control over what happened in my life. The right for someone to tell or not tell people what has happened to them is hugely important to someone's healing. This can help or hinder someone feeling control over their life. Telling people what happened was my right and mine alone. The Dean violated me by taking this away from me. Perhaps if the Dean had really cared, he would have discussed the option of me telling my parents and maybe this would have led me to tell them. I know things would have been different if my right to tell them hadn't been stolen. I couldn't handle my dad being there, because it was not my choice. I had two men making decisions for me.

After going to court and being ridiculed by the judge for not going to the police even though Noah had "ejaculated", I couldn't stand to be near my dad. I was embarrassed, ashamed, and angry. My dad may not have been in the actual courtroom, but he was there in court and with no one else around I pointed my anger towards him.

He was going to be spending another night in Chicago and he spoke to me about getting dinner. When we got back to my dorm, I refused to sign him, beyond caring what the Dean would do to me. My dad said he had left a bag in my room, so I went up to retrieve it, came back down, threw it at his feet and didn't even say bye. I feel so terrible about the way I treated my dad when he wanted to help me. I wish that things hadn't happened this way, though I do think that having that Order of Protection was a good thing.

I also wish that through this situation my school and my parents had taken the time to talk through my options with me, instead of telling me what to do. I was told not to go to the police. I was told that I should do a hearing through the school. I was told that I had to go to court. What my school did was for their own benefit. Schools don't want rape to tarnish their reputation. In contrast, I know what my dad did was, in his mind, for my benefit. But maybe if I had been asked if I wanted to go to court and had the process explained to me, I would have chosen to go anyway. And then it would have been my choice.

I love my parents and I know they want what is best for me. When I sat in the laundry room in my dorm contemplating suicide, I called my parents. I told them that there was a case against me.

"Please, just let me come home. I don't want to be here anymore."

"If you come home though, you'll miss your finals," my mom said.

"Please, Mommy, just let me come home."

"I know things are hard now, but your finals will be over soon and you can come home then."

I wish that my parents had just let me come home then. I know that they didn't keep me at school to hurt me. They didn't know I was suicidal and really, I don't know what the Dean told them.

If you know someone who has been raped or assaulted, the worst thing you can do is make decisions for them. Their right to make a decision was violently taken from them and forcing them to go to the police or court is detrimental to their healing. It has to be their choice. It is also detrimental if someone is in distress and you do not take this seriously. I am not saying this to call out my parents, but to help anyone who is in a similar situation and does not know what to do. If I had gone home, I don't know if things would have been better for me. Going home probably would have meant dropping out, but it would be better to be a college dropout than dead. I cannot change anything that happened in the past, but I can recognize that my parents did what they did out of care for me. That's not something I can say about the Dean.

# CHAPTER 8

## Sarah

Sarah and I met our freshman year of high school. It was geometry class and I was annoyed every time she would try to speak to me during class. Didn't she know that was against the rules? Sarah had the inexplicable ability to eat lunch with the quiet outcasts (me) and still smoke cigarettes and go to parties with the cool kids. Her refusal to adhere to a single social group threatened the popular clique and people either loved or hated her. First, they hated her because she was chubby, but a bout of anorexia quickly fixed that. Then they hated her because there were rumors that she got with a bunch of guys. You can either be a "prude" or a "slut" in high school and each comes with its own set of pros and cons. Sarah lived far away and was able to go to my high school because one of her parents worked for the town. Our friendship had been solidified during a sleepover freshman year, right before Halloween. We had watched *Child's Play, The Grudge, and Silent Hill.* I had never seen a scary movie before and her knowledge and lack of fear was intoxicating.

Through high school our friendship got stronger and by senior year she was practically living at my house. We shared all of our secrets and she tried to introduce me to alcohol, something that terrified and thrilled me. We did things any pair of girlfriends do. We shopped, talked about boys, baked, took hilarious pictures, and made videos, including our own cooking show. We went snowshoeing and zip-lined in New Hampshire and we swam in the pond by her house. I helped her with her writing and I envied the way she never did her homework, but did better than me on math tests. We had an intricate web of inside jokes and we were Sarah and Laurie.

Sarah and I took every class we could together, from photography to algebra and women's history. I even rearranged my schedule and dropped yoga senior year in order to take tennis, the much more physically demanding class, just so we could take drama together. We even ran a toiletry drive together, for a homeless shelter called the Pine Street Inn.

One night during a sleepover, we lay on a blanket in the field behind her house and looked up the stars. The sky was mostly clear, with a veil of clouds sweeping across our view. It looked like a poster of the Milky Way that you might see in a science classroom. We were far from the city, so the stars were bright and proud. We had just had a fight and I had locked myself in her bathroom. When I had eventually come out of the bathroom, neither of us had apologized. Instead we just went outside.

Senior year, I took a class called African American History, and we went to a museum to see an exhibit about the eugenics movement. On the ride back to school, a group of boys in the class started making fun of Sarah. They couldn't handle the way she dressed and her "I don't give a shit" attitude. I was shocked that they would make fun of her with me sitting right there. Didn't they know she was my best friend? I didn't say a thing to them and I felt terribly guilty for not standing up for her. I've always hated confrontation and, in the moment, I didn't know what to do.

Sarah was slightly taller than me and had long brown hair. She was adamant that we both had green eyes, but hers were hazel and more brown than anything else. Most things didn't bother her.

One day I told her that she had "raccoon eyes" from smudged mascara.

"Never say that to me again."

"It's not a big deal, it happens to everyone."

"Alice and her friends used to tell me I had raccoon eyes. I don't want to hear that ever again."

"I'm sorry, I didn't know."

Maybe her "I don't give a shit" attitude was really an act, and she was as insecure as the rest of us.

Any time I told Sarah that I liked a guy, she somehow ended up getting with him. And when I told her that I wanted a prom dress with rosettes, I only had to open Facebook to see a picture of the dress she had bought for herself, exactly as I had described. I made excuses for her and thought the bond we shared was worth it.

When applying for college, Sarah was dead set on a large university in Chicago. I had applied to other places, but at the last minute I decided to apply there too. Being in Chicago was a big deal for me. I knew I wanted to go to school in a big city. The school had an amazing teacher education program. It was the only place I had looked at that had you start internships in real classrooms during your first weeks of freshman year, and Sarah being there would be a huge bonus. When we both got in and decided to go there, I was ridiculously excited. By chance, Sarah and I ended up in the same dorm and on the same floor, the fourth floor. It was an all-girls floor and this gave us the name "fourth floor whores."

I think Sarah resented that her lame friend from high school had tagged along to college. We had different ideas of what this new space would mean for our friendship. When she saw my dorm room for the first time she could only say, "Wow. This is a lot smaller than my room, like a lot smaller. And it smells like a hamster."

We ended up in different orientation groups, so I didn't see her much for the first week. That first weekend, though, we had plans to go to the Lincoln Park Zoo. It's a pretty awesome place to visit, and free. I wore my Urban Outfitters cream dress that I had bought with a Hanukkah gift card and my Marc Jacobs bag that had been a joint 18th birthday and high school graduation present. Sarah and I perused the zoo, visiting the monkeys and big cats, and it felt like we were okay. It started raining and we snagged some garbage bags from the bathroom to use as ponchos. I didn't want to get wet, but I was mostly paranoid about destroying my bag. Sarah then got a text from Paul. She had met him in her orientation group and she had a thing for him.

"Can you please stop looking at your phone," I asked her timidly.

"It's Paul, hold on a minute," she responded as we took shelter under an awning.

I was getting annoyed, but I didn't want a fight.

"Paul wants to hang out, so I'm gonna go meet him!"

"Wait, are you being serious? I thought we were going to get lunch."

"Yeah, but Paul and I have been getting really close and I really need to see him."

So she left me at the zoo, in the rain, wearing a trash bag, to go hang out with him. But I couldn't even be mad at her. Hurt, maybe, but she was popular already and getting just a bit of her time was something.

The next weekend Sarah would end up getting alcohol poisoning, and some guys at the party would bring her to the hospital. Sarah met Ryan at this party and he was one of the guys who brought her to the hospital. I was jealous that I hadn't been a part of that night, clinging to her every word as she described the story of waking up in the hospital and flirting with another alcohol poisoning patient. Her hospital ID band had mistakenly printed that she was born in 1983 instead of 1993. She then came up with a plan to get more alcohol. She would use her hospital ID band to prove her age and explain to the clerk at a store that she had lost her wallet when she was at the hospital, so that's why she didn't have her ID.

The corner store a couple blocks from 1453 happily bought her story. That's how cool Sarah was, she could turn alcohol poisoning into a way to score more alcohol. On September 17, her hospital band got us a bag full of Four Lokos.

Earlier in that week, Sarah's mother had sent her a vacuum in the mail and I had helped her lug it across campus from the mailroom to our dorm. Two guys had come along, Fred and Tony. They carried the vacuum the rest of the way to our dorm and even up the four flights of stairs. When Tony revealed that they lived in 1453 and gave Sarah his number, we felt we had received a golden ticket.

Paul invited her to a party that Saturday night and she invited me. My first college party! I was one of the cool kids! We were pre-gaming in Paul's dorm when the RA showed up. While we pre-gamed, Paul's friend texted to tell him that he had broken his ankle jumping a fence. I thought about how much that sucked and how long it would take to heal.

When we were still too drunk to go back to the dorm and getting cold in the playground, Sarah texted Tony. We went to his apartment with two of the guys we were hanging out with. That night at Noah's apartment, I felt like an outsider. I had been in the bathroom when everyone was getting settled in the living room and that left me with nowhere to sit, so I leaned against the wall, feeling like I wanted to go to the dorm and sleep. Sarah had handed me a rum and Coke and I tentatively sipped it, just wanting to fit in. When Noah started talking to me, I felt special. When everything was over, and Sarah and the guys came back, I was in shock and intense physical pain. Noah told them that while they were out he had taken care of me. Sarah thanked him, and it was like living in a nightmare. I asked her if we could leave and she was adamant that they were going to watch a movie and she was going to stay. Tony opened his Garfield piggy bank and gave me some money for a taxi back to the dorm, so I left alone. Sarah later told me that that night after I left, Noah went for a run.

Maybe a year or so later it occurred to me that I had been in a taxi, so I could have gone anywhere. Hospital. Police. Airport. Anywhere. Maybe you are thinking that now too. I can assure you that in those moments I was in shock and the only thought in my head was "get back to the dorm."

The next day is hard to remember, but certain things stick out. After my shower, I had fallen into a restless sleep with my contacts in, and when I opened my eyes they were dry and practically glued shut. My skin felt foreign and dirty, so I removed my contacts and took another shower. That day, I wore my glasses and for clothing I wore a hoodie and loose sweatpants because of the pain. I had a terrible hangover and my head was throbbing. For most of the day I felt on the verge of throwing up. The weird thing about Plan B at many pharmacies is that, though it's supposed to be available over the counter, you still have to ask the pharmacist for it. It was awkward to buy, but I'm just so grateful I was able to take it. I cannot explain the relief I felt when I got my period a couple of weeks later.

I saw Sarah in the afternoon and told her that something had happened with Noah. She just thought I had consented and that I now regretted it.

"It sounds like you had sex with him and now you wish you hadn't," she chided me.

I couldn't admit to her or myself what had really happened and maybe it was like that. I thought to myself, *you did something that you now regret, and that's why you're upset.*

The first few weeks of college had been a hard adjustment. I think it is for a lot of people. I was so homesick. I missed seeing my friends every day, watching TV and talking with my mom, and just knowing the ins and outs of school and home. I was friendly with some people from my classes and dorm, but I wouldn't say I had made any real friends.

As you can see, I wasn't very social before that night, but after it, it was hard to get myself to do just about anything. Sarah was flourishing, always with friends and going to the next party. She and Paul probably hooked up, but they never dated and after that night I never saw him or the other people we were with again. Paul's apparent disinterest in her didn't seem to bother her, she just found new people to hang out with and new guys to be with. I'm not trying to shame her; girls are allowed to enjoy being with guys. I'm just sharing what happened.

I missed Sarah terribly and was overjoyed anytime she came to my dorm room to watch a movie or just hang out. Maybe I relied on her too much, but at the time she was my only friend. She told me how she ran into Noah on the street and he had asked about me and for my number. I wasn't sure if she was being serious or joking, but I was relieved that she hadn't given it to him.

A few days before Halloween, Sarah and I were supposed to see a screening of the new Justin Timberlake movie, *In Time*. I had assumed it would be just the two of us, but at the last minute Sarah told me she invited a girl named Sylvie. I want to believe that I was okay with Sarah having other friends. This had never bothered me in high school, but I hadn't left the dorm for anything but school in weeks and I wasn't in the mood to share Sarah. I told Sarah that I didn't want to go to the movie anymore. In the hall of our dorm, in front of other students, she started screaming at me.

"You're such an immature baby! All you ever want is attention!"

I didn't respond to her; I just started crying and ran back to my room. That night she sent me a Facebook message detailing all of the reasons we shouldn't be friends. She wrote out 26 reasons, labeling them A–Z. In short, I was immature, judgemental, and needy. A couple of days later I had my first meeting with the Dean, and my depression and anxiety was overwhelming.

# CHAPTER 9

## *Sour*

I was a sour child. I had a lovely childhood, so I had no real reason to be so sour. I grew up in Boston. My dad owned his own hardware store and my mom made jewelry and stayed at home, so I rarely even had a babysitter. I loved school and I went to a Montessori school nearby. I had my sister as my playmate and bickering partner and my best friend Emily, lived right around the corner. I zipped around the city on my Razor scooter and I was never lonely or bored. I was just sour. Not all the time – I was happy a lot too – but I was keenly aware of my emotions. I never wanted to smile in pictures, because I didn't want to give the picture taker the satisfaction of making me smile for the camera. My parents even had a friend paint my portrait, and now for all eternity a close-up of my sullen face is immortalized on canvas. I get to see it every time I visit them.

One afternoon, when I was in kindergarten, I went to my friend Erin's house for a playdate. She and her au pair walked me back to school, so my mom could pick me up there. We raced down the street and I was ecstatic that I was beating her. I was so into the thrill of winning that I didn't notice I had run right through wet cement. My beautiful patent leather Mary Janes were ruined.

*Aged 6, in Monterey Bay, California – refusing to smile at the camera!*

When we got to the school my mom was there and so was a man who was doing a story on the school for a newspaper. He wanted to take our picture and I was not about to do that. I refused. I was embarrassed and upset about my shoes and I didn't want to make myself smile for the camera. Maybe other kids could have sucked it up or not been so bothered, but I wasn't like that.

When I was 13, my family moved a whole mile to the suburb of Brookline. Brookline is like the Lincoln Park of Boston, but it's not part of the city. It's a lovely town with great shopping, restaurants, and parks. In Boston our house was tall, but narrow. My family lived on the first three floors and my parents rented out the top two floors. My parents were tired of being landlords and I was being bullied in school. A move to Brookline had been in order.

I'm not saying that being sour is a gateway to depression, but by middle school it was hard for me to get out of bed and everything felt heavy. Sometimes depression is triggered by something specific and sometimes it just happens. I felt emotions so strongly and if I was sad, I was sad. My depression would come and go, hitting me with a vengeance in tenth grade.

I even missed some school because of it. I had been okay for about two years by the time I started college, but what happened that September night triggered depression and anxiety like I had never experienced. Nothing I did gave me any joy and I lost interest in most things. I couldn't get excited about anything because nothing felt like it mattered. I had never had panic attacks before and they scared me. I used alcohol to cope, but it only made me feel worse.

As I have mentioned, I went to the gym every day for hours and I was also obsessed with what I ate. It made me feel better to go to bed every night feeling hungry. Exercising and fixating on what I ate gave me a sense of control over my life. I couldn't control what would happen with my case or anything surrounding that. I had had control ripped away from me that night and I was spiraling.

I also became obsessed with my grades and nothing less than an A would do. My freshman year, I got a B+ in rhetoric and a B in freshman philosophy. Rhetoric, to me, was my disaster class, but in philosophy I got A's on all of my assignments. I guess I missed too many classes and, with no excuse from the Dean, I was out of luck. In a sea of A's I had two B's, and B became synonymous with failure. I know a B is not even a bad grade, but at the time, I was obsessed.

Grades were another thing that I had control over, but it wasn't just that. I felt that I needed to prove myself and show my school that they were wrong about me. Over the years I passed on hanging out with friends and sleeping just to make sure I would never fail, but I never felt proud. An A was never enough. If I got a 98 on an assignment, why wasn't it a 100?

This is how committed I was to school: I went to class when my grandpa was being taken off life support and started crying while I gave a presentation on teaching paragraph structure to third graders. I pushed through that presentation and got my A. During my time at school, my self-esteem was shot and I had never-ending anxiety about my schoolwork.

My sister was a senior in college when I was a freshman. She went to a small liberal arts school in upstate New York, the exact opposite of my school. When she graduated, I took a flight home to Boston on the Thursday night, drove to New York with my parents on Friday, and was back in Chicago by Sunday. No way was I going to miss any classes. After her graduation, we had a small party in her campus apartment. It was my immediate family, my grandparents, and a smattering of aunts, uncles, and one cousin. At the graduation party were Sun Chips. I had eaten only eggs and salad for months. I ate a Sun Chip and it broke the seal. I couldn't starve myself anymore; it was destroying my body. And when I tasted that Sun Chip, I knew I couldn't go back to my dangerous eating habits. I had become so obsessed with exercising that I had abused my body to the point that I would not be able to run for about a year after injuring my hip during that spring. Things got pretty bad when I had the case against me, but the summer after my freshman year I worked on figuring out how to be healthy. It wasn't easy or completely possible to do this alone.

I think of all the people I tried to reach out to for help over the years – professors and more. I went to my doctor during the summer after freshman year because I'd injured my hip from overuse. When she saw how much weight I had lost, she just complimented me. I had gone from a healthy BMI to a healthy BMI on the cusp of underweight. She didn't make the connection that I had an overuse injury and had lost so much weight over a short amount of time. If she had asked me some questions and shown an interest in why I was injured and had lost so much weight, maybe I could have gotten help sooner. I really wonder why people don't help each other when it seems so obvious that someone needs help.

I knew I needed better ways to cope, but it would be a few years before I found them.

# CHAPTER 10

## Mailbox Key

The mailroom at my school was in the Student Center. Mine was mailbox 1080 and I shared it with my two roommates. To get into the mailbox, I had to use a tiny key that I kept with my other keys on the lobster keychain that my grandma had bought me. When I first saw my roommate's mail in my mailbox, I thought it was a mistake.

"One of my roommates has mail in my mailbox," I told one of the guys working in the mailroom.

"Yeah, that's for you to share," he replied.

What can I say? No one told me.

During Noah's sham one-week suspension, I went to the mailroom to check my mail. Just a few months earlier, Sarah and I had gone to the same mailroom to pick up her vacuum. Freshman year, I would check my mail about once a week. The only things I was ever sent were things from my mom, the occasional Amazon order, and of course my lovely postcard from The Cook County Courthouse. Since I shared the mailbox with my roommates, I was worried that one of them had seen the postcard, but at this point it didn't matter.

That day during Noah's suspension, I checked my mail. I didn't feel safe at the Student Center, but I still had to go on with my life. I didn't have any mail, so I left the mailroom and started walking down the back staircase. There was Noah, walking up the stairs. He didn't say a word, he just stared at me. There was no one else on the stairs and I wanted to turn around, but that would mean going in the direction he was headed. We passed each other on the stairs, as he continued to stare me down. I ran back to the dorm and didn't feel safe to leave for the rest of the day. I thought about emailing the Dean about what had happened, but I knew it wouldn't make any difference.

That summer, a few weeks after I got the email about being responsible for blah blah blah you know what I'm talking about, I got another email fining me for not turning in my mailbox key. Fighting this injustice became my raison d'être. Find me responsible for pretending to be raped and I'll get angry, but how dare you accuse me of not turning in my mailbox key? Maybe it was displacement or some other pretentious psychological term, but I'd be damned if they were going to think I was the type of person to not turn in my key. How could I kill myself now? I was going to be fined a whole $20. How unfair would that be! I emailed to explain that I had turned it in and I was ready for a fight. Here's my super formal, pissed-off email:

> To whom it may concern,
> I absolutely turned in both my room key and mailbox key on June 8th at approximately 1.00pm. I placed both keys in the university supplied envelope and I placed the envelope in the key return slot in my dorm's lobby. I was therefore quite surprised to receive an email stating that I had not returned my mailbox key. I immediately called housing services and spoke with a very friendly representative who explained to me that this was the first year the dorms were collecting mailbox keys and this must have been a glitch. I hope this issue is resolved soon.
> Thank you,
> Laurie Katz

You go, past Laurie! Stick it to housing services!

Two days later, they emailed back and said it must have been a mistake. *Wait, so you thought I hadn't turned it in, but*

*I told you I did, and now you believe me?* I was relieved and pissed off. What happened with the key showed me it was possible to change things. I thought, *why had I been able to fight that mailbox key injustice, but not for something so much more important?*

I never seriously considered transferring colleges. I don't know why, but I was determined that if I was going to finish college, it would be at my school. Transferring would be admitting that something bad had happened to me and that I wasn't okay. Through everything I still couldn't face that he had raped me, and transferring was like saying, "I was raped." The "mailbox key incident" fueled the fire in me to change the letter in my file, and this would consume me on and off for years.

# CHAPTER 11

## Sarah Part Two

After winter break freshman year, I ran into Sarah in the Student Center when I was getting lunch. I started crying and told her, "I don't want to not be friends anymore." We hugged and things went back to the way they were. I think I apologized, but she never did. I just couldn't handle doing everything alone and a poor friend felt better than nothing. I eventually told her about how I was doing a case against Noah, but she was less than supportive.

When Sarah had no better plans, she hung out with me. And when something better came along, she left. I started going to parties with her and stopped caring about what happened to me.

My partying was getting out of control and by the spring of my sophomore year, I realized that I was going to die if I didn't stop. At this time, Sarah's partying was beyond out of control and it scared me. She made a new friend, Laura. Our similar names only made things worse. Sarah met Laura at a party and Laura was into hardcore drugs. I couldn't get Sarah to see that she was a bad influence, so I dissociated myself from Sarah. I had made friends and I couldn't be around that partying lifestyle anymore.

In March, for Sarah's 20th birthday, she had a party. Let me rephrase that. Sarah was the only person I knew who could justify having two parties for her 20th birthday. One on Thursday night and one on Saturday night. I didn't want to go to either of them, but I couldn't let her down. This was her birthday, after all. Laura had introduced her to a guy named John and he and his friends had a condo in a high-rise downtown. They rented it out for parties and provided the drugs and alcohol to underage girls, for a fee. Sarah's parties were in this condo. As a friend of John's, she got it for free.

At the first party, Sarah got ridiculously drunk. I had decided not to drink that night and it was uncomfortable to watch everyone at the party go through the stages of getting progressively more wasted. One of the people who came to the party was Ryan, and when Sarah starting swaying he helped me carry her to the bedroom and turn her on her side when she began throwing up. I was so afraid she would choke on her vomit and die. There was this guy, Aaron, a friend of John's, who was all over her and it creeped me out. He was one of the guys who would rent the condo for parties and he gave me a bad feeling.

I had my internship in the morning, so I couldn't stay late. When some more of our friends who I trusted arrived and took over looking out for Sarah, I left, feeling like at least I knew Ryan had her best interests at heart. The next day, I met up with Sarah and told her what had happened and how worried I was.

"You really scared me last night. You were throwing up and I thought you were going to choke on your vomit. I really thought you were going to die."

"I can't believe you would even bring that up. Why are you trying to make me feel bad? It sounds like you're just jealous of my party."

I wanted to yell at her. How dare she accuse me of being jealous, when I was just trying to help? And really, I wasn't jealous. I thought back to the times I had felt left out and envious of her when she had gone to parties without me. I had felt jealous to miss the night she got alcohol poisoning. How ridiculous is that? I had wanted to be a part of these crazy and hilarious stories she told me. It wasn't hilarious or fun anymore. Her drinking didn't make her cool, it made her ... sad. *But*, Sarah could never take criticism and I knew I was losing her with this conversation, so I swallowed my pride and apologized.

"I'm sorry, I don't mean to make you feel bad. I just want to make sure you're okay."

"Well, I'm having another party on Saturday night. I want you to come, but if you're going to be a wet blanket, don't."

When her second party rolled around on Saturday, I knew I had to go to make sure she was okay. At this party, she was drunk and high and screaming at everyone. I tried to talk to her and tell her how much she was hurting herself, but she just laughed. This, coupled with the fact that some of the people at the party made me feel unsafe, made me realize the best thing for me to do was to leave. We had some other friends at the party who I trusted to make sure she was okay, but I later found out that they got fed up and left too. Sometimes I wish I had stayed, and sometimes I would feel like I had let her down (like she had let me down leaving me at Noah's), but while you should do your best to look out for friends, sometimes your safety needs to be a priority. You cannot control the actions of another person.

On the train ride home, I thought I saw Noah on the platform of one of the stops. As the train pulled into the station, I locked eyes with this man. Close up it was clear it was not Noah, but my panic from thinking it was him and the stress of the night caught up with me and I started crying on the train. All the things that had happened since Sarah and I had come to Chicago had broken me, and it felt like now Sarah was broken too.

I didn't hear from Sarah for about two weeks. Then out of nowhere, she texted me and wanted to meet up to get cupcakes. We went to Molly's Cupcakes, the same place we had gone with our friend Aurora on my 19th birthday. When I saw Sarah, I was surprised that she was with Aaron. Aaron left the cupcake store soon after I arrived, and Sarah and I went back to my apartment with our cupcakes. She told me that the night of her party (the second one) she had hit rock bottom. Aaron had told her that if she said a few words she would be a part of his religion, and everything she had ever done would be forgiven. She didn't apologize for anything. In her mind the devil was everywhere and he had made her do it.

After knowing Aaron for two weeks, she had moved out of her university apartment and in with him. Sarah had adopted this new religion. It doesn't matter what the religion was. Any religion can be harmful when it is taken to a level that takes away your freedom. She no longer believed in evolution or that gay people didn't choose to be so. It was okay for a man to physically abuse his wife if the circumstances deemed it necessary, and the devil controlled everything. She believed that I was going to hell and that I needed to join this religion too. I made it clear to her that that would never happen, and this upset her. I tried to be supportive and to help if I could. We hung out a few times and I told her delicately what I thought. I listened to her justify her new life.

My apartment building had a roof deck that gave a view of downtown from Lincoln Park, where I was. I always marveled at how small the high-rises looked, even though people were eating and peeing and having fights and making up inside them. It looked like a Lego city. One night, Sarah and I went up there. I could see Lake Michigan glimmering in the moonlight and it was getting cold. That afternoon, Polly and I had visited Sarah at her new apartment, which was a long bus ride away. We had seen how Aaron treated her. It was like she was his slave, waiting on him and needing his permission to leave the apartment and come back to Lincoln Park with us.

Sarah and I had different majors and interests in college, so we never took any classes together. We were supposed to take women's physical health together, since we both needed to take a science class with a lab, but it started at 8.00am and Sarah told me that she had to be home to wake Aaron up and make his breakfast. Aaron and Sarah were also each incredibly self-righteous about the fact that they did not drink or do drugs, while Aaron simultaneously made money with his party business, selling just that.

On the roof of my building, I tried to understand what had led Sarah to be with Aaron. Sarah always needed something to belong to. Every week was a new cause, even if it contradicted what she had been fighting for the week prior. Being with Aaron gave her security and a sense of purpose. He had a lot of friends who welcomed her, and I guess she needed to feel accepted. Now Sarah was dancing on the edge of the roof, looking down into the alley.

"Sarah, please come back from there. You're scaring me."

"It doesn't matter if I die. If I die, I know now I'll go to heaven."

After convincing her to come away from the edge and get back inside to my apartment, she told me she and Aaron were planning on getting married. There were two main reasons that they needed to do this. To have sex in her new religion, Aaron had told her, they would have to be man and wife. The next reason was that Aaron was on a student visa that was running out. Getting married could keep him in the country.

I knew that I had to do whatever it took to stop this wedding from happening.

I called our old boss, Tim, from an organization we had both worked for in high school. I decided that I needed "adult" help with this one, and at 19 I did not feel equipped. Tim was knowledgeable about religions and cultures, and I trusted him. He agreed that what was happening wasn't true to the religion, but it was her choice and it seemed like she was happy. This pissed me off. I called her mom and she didn't seem too worried either. No one was there to see how bad it was.

One day our friend Aurora told me that Sarah had never shown up when they had lunch plans and I was freaked out. I called Sarah and a woman picked up and told me, "Sarah doesn't want to talk to you. Never call this number again." A man then took over on the phone and relayed the same message.

I continued to get threatening phone calls telling me to stay away from her, and someone tried to break into my apartment. They even ripped the Mezuzah from my doorpost. I saw Sarah one more time, but things weren't right. After that, I never saw her again.

During the summer after sophomore year, I had a minor health scare that turned out to be nothing. In desperate need of my best friend, I called Sarah. It was easier on the phone to pretend things were normal, but she didn't sound like the Sarah I knew and loved. She was adamant that this was a just punishment for something I had done and that she was grateful it wasn't happening to her.

She would message me on Facebook in the summer after junior year. She and Aaron were married and it was too toxic to know her. I didn't respond, so she unfriended me. When I mention Sarah now, either I say that we grew apart or that she joined a cult. Both are true in their own way.

# CHAPTER 12

# Closet Full of Memories

In high school, Sarah and I became obsessed with a brand called Free People. Free People makes beautiful overpriced clothing that presents an air of bohemia with a splash of the Great Depression. There was a Free People store that Sarah and I would go to on weekends and try on the clothing, fantasizing about the lives we would lead if we could only get the wardrobe to match. We once ran into our woman's history teacher, and it was jarring to see her out and having a life – news flash: teachers are people too! I did end up buying one top with a mix of birthday money and calling my dad to use my emergency credit card, with a promise to pay him back. Sarah and I called this shirt my "Aria top" because it looked like something that Aria on our favorite TV show, *Pretty Little Liars,* would wear. The irony of that is only getting to me now.

During my freshman orientation week, my group went to a neighborhood of Chicago called Wicker Park. Wicker Park is an impossibly cool area with thrift shops, bars, and high-end stores like Marc Jacobs and Alexis Bittar. When I went with my orientation group, I knew that I wanted to bring Sarah there, so when we hung out on September 17th, that's where we went.

With my orientation group we had taken the train there, but this time Sarah and I had it in our heads that we would walk.

We didn't have smartphones with Google Maps yet, so we looked up the directions on her computer and decided it didn't look too complicated. After walking for about a half an hour we asked a woman on the street if we were we heading in the right direction. We weren't. We went back the way we came and began Laurie and Sarah's Wicker Park Adventure Take Two. Walking to Wicker Park, we talked about everything: boys, our orientation groups, how terrible the internet was in the dorm, everything. We laughed at the absurdity of a church having a fall festival, as our sweat and dehydration pointed to it still being summer. We walked through the Ukrainian Village, but as we were coming from Lincoln Park, this turned out to be the least direct route. We decided we were lost again, so Sarah said we should ask for directions. There was no one on the street to ask, so she dragged me into a bar. I was afraid we would get in trouble for going inside, but Sarah was so confident that no one questioned our right to be there. It was about three in the afternoon and bar was near empty. A man in his thirties sat at the bar and I thought it was strange that this normal looking guy was drinking alone, in an empty bar, on a Saturday afternoon. He assured us that if we kept walking on Western Ave, we would get to Wicker Park.

We were going to the party that night, the one that Paul had invited Sarah to, and I needed something that wasn't from The Gap or Ann Taylor Loft. I thought about the Aria top, but I wanted something new. In a thrift store called Buffalo Exchange, there it was. A greyish off-white Free People top with lovely lace and a wide neckline. It was inexpensive and perfect. I bought the shirt and got excited for the night. The neckline wasn't particularly low, but it was just wide enough to show my bra straps, so I had to wear a strapless bra. I had exactly one of those. It was nude, from Victoria's Secret Pink, and I had bought it to wear with my prom dress. I had ended up with a hot pink dress with thin straps after I couldn't get the rosette dress I wanted.

I am not including this because I think what I was wearing that night particularly matters. I could have been wearing a burlap sack and I still would have been raped. This is just a part of the story and it's my story, so I can include whatever I want. Also, think of all the countries where women wear saris or burkas and rape is still prevalent. What someone was wearing is just a ridiculous excuse.

I splashed on my favorite perfume, Coco Chanel. It was a gift from my grandma the previous Christmas and I loved how grown-up I felt when I wore it. I wore jeans and black leather boots too. The jeans are long gone. I probably got rid of them when my dorm did a clothing drive at the end of the school year. I love the boots, and though I feel a little weird wearing them, they are too beautiful to give up.

For a time, I continued to wear my lovely grey Free People top. If I could wear it then I was okay, and nothing bad had happened to me. I wore the bra too, trying to forget what I had said. Then, one day, I just couldn't do it anymore. I was never able to wear the perfume again. The smell did too good a job of bringing me back to Noah's bedroom. But, I still have the top and the bra and the perfume too. They survived four years of college and my move back to Boston. They're in my room as I write this, and though I can't wear or use them, I can't bring myself to get rid of them either.

The perfume was expensive, but it's not just that. I don't want to lose anything else important to me to that night. It was a gift from my grandma who died on Easter in 2016 and now it's harder than ever to get rid of anything she bought me. The shirt made me feel beautiful and confident. It now sticks out against my teacher wardrobe. I know I'll never wear it again, but it's a memory of Sarah and a reminder to honor the 18-year-old girl who did what she had to.

The bra is another thing. Bras are wickedly expensive. I have a grand total of zero things in my everyday wardrobe that warrant a strapless bra, but if by chance I need one, I'm ready!

My mom has my prom dress on a dress form mannequin in my parents' laundry room, but when will I ever need to wear a prom dress again? That lovely top? Well, that's not going to be worn either, so no luck there with the strapless bra. I put the bra in the trash once, but quickly rescued it.

I have these things just taking up space in my life, but I tell myself that should I need them, there they are. I struggle with what these objects mean and what it might mean to get rid of them. If I hold on to them, does that mean I'm fine because I can potentially use them? Or am I only okay if I get rid of them and stop having an emotional attachment to the things I wore on the worst night of my life? Maybe they are a part of my story, and maybe they act as the only witnesses to that night and my only proof to myself that that night happened. The clothing and the perfume were there and I was too, and so was Noah. And if I can remember what I wore and those things still exist, then everything else is true too.

Or maybe I just have trouble getting rid of things.

I think we are all guilty of keeping clothing and objects that we know we will never use, but we just can't seem to get rid of. I don't have the answers, just a closet full of memories.

# CHAPTER 13

## Physical Pain

Though I have difficulty remembering every detail of my rape, my body remembers it all. While my brain struggled to help me survive and gave me the peace of freezing, my body was present the entire time. The physical pain that started that night stayed with me for years. If you've never heard of vaginismus, you're not alone. I had never heard of it either. This lovely affliction also goes by the name genito-pelvic pain penetration disorder. I wish it had a different name that was less awkward to say and write. In the weeks after my rape, the bruises and bitemarks faded, but this pain did not go away. It would get better for a time, but would never leave me. The pain was unbearable at night when my panic set in, and it was my constant companion. Some people feel the pain with vaginismus when they try to have sex, use tampons, or have a pelvic exam. I felt it all the time. Vaginismus is kind of like a reflex, like your eye shutting quickly whenever anything goes near it. Vaginismus tried to protect me, but my body was on constant red alert and I was afraid that something was seriously wrong with me. I almost didn't include vaginismus in this story, but many women experience vaginismus after sexual crimes. It's never talked about, but it's incredibly common. So, if this is happening to you, it's not permanent and you're not crazy.

After my rape, I didn't go to the doctor. I don't even feel like justifying that now, so I won't. In the summer after my freshman year, the pain was scaring me and I wanted to make sure I didn't have any STDs. I went to every girl's favorite place, the gynecologists. I had never been before and I was extremely nervous. Not just because of what would happen, but because I was afraid to face that being raped may have damaged me. And what if nothing could be done about that? In the exam room, I sat in my paper gown and waited for the doctor. When she came in she just wanted to get started. I didn't feel like a person, but just another patient to get through. I made myself voice my concerns to her and told her that I had been sexually assaulted. Saying "sexually assaulted" feels better than saying "raped" for whatever reason, and it's still hard for me to say the words, "I was raped."

The doctor confirmed that I had vaginismus, and that "sometimes that just happens."

She told me that it might hurt during the exam and to let her know if it did. When she started, the pain was unbearable. Fragments of memories had been stored away and I wasn't in her office anymore. I was on Noah's bed with his knees keeping me from being able to close my legs. I squeezed my nails into my palm to try to remind myself of where I was and that I was safe. As I became more aware, I realized I was crying. I managed to say to the doctor, "That really hurts."

Her response was, "It doesn't hurt, it's just uncomfortable." And she continued what she was doing. When the exam was over, I couldn't stop shaking as I got dressed. A few days later I found out that I didn't have any STDs, so that was a relief.

I usually don't suffer with that pain anymore, but when it does come back it's a reminder of what my body had to endure. I got so used to it always being there that when it comes back it surprises me, and I feel compassion for my past self and what I went through.

A few years later I did my research and found an amazing gynecologist who listens to my concerns and takes my rape seriously. The next time I had an exam, my new doctor talked me through the process and was gentle and kind. There are good people out there who believe victims and don't cause more harm. They can be harder to find, but they do exist. If someone had broken my arm, I wouldn't think twice about sharing that information, so why should I need to hide and feel shame for the actions of another person? I spent a long time not caring about my physical or mental health, but I have learned to honor my feelings and to not be ashamed of my pain.

CHAPTER 14

# The Suburbs

My dad's cousin lives in the suburbs of Chicago. I usually refer to her as my cousin because it makes things less complicated. I met her when my dad and I went to visit my school right after I was accepted. I wore my purple shirt (the one I would later wear to my hearing), when the three of us went out for brunch. My mom is Protestant and my dad is Jewish, so I have been raised as both. I went to my cousin's house for every Rosh Hashanah, Yom Kippur, and Passover when I was going to school in Chicago. I was welcomed by her family at every event and she did the same for my sister when she eventually moved to Chicago.

In my life, I have never been the biggest fan of the suburbs. I know that for many people the suburbs are amazing places to live and if you like living in the suburbs, that's great. I don't like a lot of things that other people like. Artificial orange juice is the main example I can think of now, but I am sure there are others.

Yes, Brookline is a suburb, but it's the least suburban suburb maybe on the planet. Growing up in Boston and then Brookline, I got accustomed to walking and taking public transportation everywhere. I didn't even get my license until I was 19 (this was after exactly one month of driving lessons and I rarely use it). It freaks me out to not have a grocery store within walking distance and my favorite (only) hobby is shopping. In a city there is always something going on and somewhere new to discover. When I was applying to colleges, I knew that I wanted a large school in a large city and this is part of what led me to my school.

By the end of my freshman year, many of the things that make me love cities were making me feel trapped in Chicago. The big buildings, congestion of people, and constant noise all added to my anxiety. With everything going on, the weekend before my hearing, I went to my cousin's house for the night. This was the day after the music festival. To get there, I took the train for about 40 minutes and she picked me up from the station. During the car ride, we drove by row after row of houses – the suburbs. Seeing that the suburbs still existed was comforting. I had been in Chicago for months, living in a nightmare for most of that time. My world had just been shattered, yet here were the suburbs as suburban as ever. I was so caught up in what was happening in my life, that it was reassuring to see the outside world was still chugging along. I don't know how I would have gotten through that time if I had not been able to go to my cousin's house. I am so grateful to her for letting me visit her that weekend and for hosting me over the years.

My excuse for going was that I needed to get out of the dorm, and this was one piece of the truth. She had no idea what was really going on. I think when you live in a dorm it can be easy to forget that houses still exist and that dorm life is not only temporary, but not fun for many people. During my visit, it was a luxury to stay in a room of my own and have a private bathroom. My cousin's fridge was stocked with different kinds of diet soda, a real treat. I tried my best to keep the hearing from my mind and my feelings of suicide faded for the day. I did my best to get some work done on my computer and I went to a craft fair with her and her husband. Sleeping was still difficult for me, but I had a TV in my room and this helped me pass the time and feel safe. I didn't hear the train rushing by my dorm room or people yelling in the halls. In the afternoon, we went to a family gathering for her son-in-law's birthday. It was all so normal.

When terrible things happen, it can be difficult to see that normality still exists. It's also a weird feeling to see that your problems don't touch different places. I do not recommend running away from your problems, but as they say, taking a step back can give perspective. Getting a change of scenery is a cliché, yes, but a good one. I still love cities and Boston is my home, but I have a special place in my heart for the suburbs now too.

# CHAPTER 15

## Storage

At the end of my freshman year, I decided to rent a small storage unit. When I say small, I mean about the size of a kitchen table. To put things in it, I had to crawl. I was going to get an apartment for the fall and it made more sense to store most of my things than to lug home extra suitcases, and it was cheaper too. When I told Sarah what I was planning, she wanted to share the storage unit with me. She said she would pay half, which she never did, and we set about putting things like our winter clothes and her vacuum into the unit. The unit was at a storage facility on Faber Ave; you could see it from Sarah's dorm window, but it was about a half a mile away. Not as far up Faber as 1453, but close. The unit was on the third floor of the facility and in a room filled with storage units piled on top of each other. There was a metal staircase on wheels that we used to get into our unit on the third level, unit D342. These were the cheapest units. There was no temperature control, a fact that the staff told us as many times as they could, (I think they just wanted us to pay extra for the temperature-controlled units). Our room was unbearably hot, but it was cheap and that's what we needed. After assessing the situation, we realized it would not be easy to get our things all the way to the unit. As we left the storage building, Sarah noticed some platform car dollies.

"We're taking these."

"I don't think we're allowed to," I said. I was waiting to hear the results of my hearing and I couldn't handle getting in trouble for anything else.

"I don't see anyone stopping us."

So, we walked down the ramp and out of the building. Sarah had told me on countless occasions that you could get away with just about anything if you looked confident enough that no one would dare question you.

We walked back to the dorm and went up to our rooms, using the elevator. This was a rare treat, as the elevator was only run during move-in and move-out. We loaded up our carts and we headed back to the storage facility. I had never noticed how slanted the sidewalk was, but on this day my cart wanted to drag me into oncoming traffic. Our carts kept getting stuck on ridges in the sidewalk and we laughed at the absurdity. It was a hot day and I was sweating pretty badly. I dreaded returning to the sauna that was our storage unit.

A few days later we had a final trip to make, and a girl named Freya came with us to help carry things. Freya lived in our dorm on the same floor as us and we were all friends. When Sarah was climbing up the metal staircase, she dropped a box on Freya's hand. Freya cut her finger pretty badly. Being the "mom" I am, I gave her a Band-Aid from my purse. It bothered me that Sarah didn't apologize, but she was too engrossed in packing the unit to capacity to notice.

I thought about my things in that unit over the summer. If I killed myself, would Sarah decide to take everything? Or would my parents care enough to have my things sent home? I had a lot of thoughts like this. *My mom just bought me all that yogurt. If I die, who will eat it?*

I did get my things out of the unit the following fall, and the lack of temperature control did nothing to harm anything.

My parents helped me get my stuff out and we drove them to my new apartment near campus. My sister moved to Chicago after her college graduation to try out a new city and we lived together. When Sarah got to Chicago a few days later she had Stan, the guy she was seeing, rent a van to drive her things less than half a mile to her university apartment. I thought this was a waste of money, but I was relieved that we wouldn't be "borrowing" any more dollies.

Freya died in a car accident the fall after I graduated. I don't think she graduated and I'm not sure what she had ended up doing with her life, but now it was over. I hadn't seen her since that day at the storage facility, and I thought about how she'd cut her finger and now she would never get a cut again. I wasn't sure how I felt. I hadn't known her too well and I hadn't seen her in years, but she was a person and it was sad and scary that her life was over, just like that. I was teaching second grade when I went on Facebook and saw all these weird posts on her wall. I usually checked my phone during lunch and I thought it was a joke, until I looked her up online and saw the news story. Dead at the scene. People still post on her wall sometimes to say how much they miss her, and it makes me sad every time.

It's strange to think about all the changes since my freshman year: the people I knew who I grew apart from and the people who died. The changes I went through and the things about myself that are still the same. I have no idea whether Sarah graduated or what her life is like now. I don't understand the point in Freya dying or in many of the things that have happened in my life. Things just happen and we have to decide if it will make us stop our lives or make a change.

# CHAPTER 16

# Nice Guys

I probably went to three parties my whole junior year of college. That spring, I was sort of seeing this guy, Tristan. We weren't boyfriend and girlfriend, a fact that he reminded me of anytime we saw each other. Tristan had dark hair and eyes. He was classically handsome and it surprised me that someone that good looking would want to be with me, even if we weren't "official." He was an inch taller than me, but we were the same height when I wore anything but flats. He treated me terribly and this felt safe. If he wasn't good to me upfront, then there would be no surprises. Tristan and I mostly hung out at his apartment, which was a long bus ride away for me, all the way in Greektown. He had a car, but he never picked me up. He never wanted to make plans in advance and if we got food, we paid separately. I do not think that one person in a relationship should pay for everything; I am just explaining the dynamic that we had. He got angry that I wouldn't have sex with him and to justify this, I told him about my rape. To him, bad things happen to everyone and it didn't make me "special."

We went about watching movies and he taught me how to play video games. Not being experienced in the dating scene, I assumed that he wasn't seeing other people. He was. He invited me to a party at his friend Molly's apartment and it happened to be around the corner from where I lived. He wanted me to meet him there, but after much debate he said he would come to my apartment and we could walk there together. It was a cold April night and Tristan and I didn't speak on the walk over. Tristan was the only person I knew at the party and he ditched me the second we arrived. I ended up sitting on the host's bed with everyone's coats. Music drifted into the room and I had an occasional visitor come in for a beer from Molly's mini fridge. I had decided not to drink that night and parties can be weird places when you're sober.

I was getting ready to leave when a guy named Harold came into the bedroom and sat down on the bed. We talked for about an hour. Harold worked in retail and was about to go on a long trip. He was a few years older than me and used to be one of the roommates at the apartment. I told him where I went to school and that I lived nearby.

"How do you know Molly?" Harold asked me.

"I know her through Tristan."

"You know Molly and Tristan used to date, right? They still hook up sometimes."

No. I hadn't known that. I was tired, bored, and hurt, so I told Harold that I was leaving.

"I'll walk you to your apartment."

"No, that's okay. I live nearby, so don't worry about it."

"What kind of guy would I be if I let a pretty girl walk home alone?"

"No, really. It's fine. You should stay and find Molly."

I didn't want Harold to know where I lived and I had no interest in him whatsoever. Girls are allowed to talk to guys with no expectation of anything. This continued, until finally I told him we could head out together, but my apartment was in the opposite direction of the train, so it wouldn't make sense for him to walk there. *We. Are. Not. Having. Sex*.

Outside Molly's apartment, I said goodbye to Harold and he asked for my number.

"Sorry, I'd rather not."

Harold didn't like that too much. He tried to kiss me and I pulled away.

"No," he said and looked genuinely confused. He tried to grab me and kiss me again. I jerked away from him.

"I thought I made it clear. I'm not interested."

"You've been talking to me for an hour and you're not interested?"

I was starting to panic. I wanted to run home, but then he'd know where I lived.

"I'm sorry, I'm not." Looking back on this, I wish I hadn't felt obligated to apologize.

He started to huff away from the building and then looked back at me. I couldn't move.

"Aren't you going home?" he asked me.

"I need to go back upstairs and find Tristan."

He looked incredulous, but thankfully he left. I waited in the building's entryway for a few minutes and then ran home.

Harold was a "nice guy". "Nice guys" have ulterior motives. I do not mean actually nice, decent guys. I'm talking about "nice guys." I'll do my best to define them here, but if you still don't know what I am talking about, you can google it. "Nice guys" believe that because they are "nice" to girls, they are owed something in return. They are martyrs. A "nice guy" is the guy who you study with, and when you won't have sex with him he gets angry and complains that, "girls never want the nice guy." Their niceness means the world owes them, and to "friendzone" a "nice guy" is the highest offense. "Nice guys" aren't really nice at all. "Nice guys" have a similar mentality to rapists. It's not about the phone number or the kiss or sex, it's about needing power over another person.

I'm happy that I stood my ground and that, though it was frightening and awkward, Harold left with nothing. Tristan had the nerve to be upset that he had seen us talking and I'm not so happy that I stuck with Tristan for a couple more months of emotional abuse. Tristan wasn't a "nice guy" but he still viewed women in the same way. He just acted on this view differently. Guys like Harold and Tristan don't see girls as individual people, but as things to use and play with. Harold felt that if he was nice to a girl, she needed to "pay him back". And Tristan … well, he just liked to collect women. If someone doesn't want to have sex with you or date you or kiss you, get over it. Being nice to a girl does not mean she owes you anything. It goes the other way too. I'm sure there are girls who are "nice girls," and manipulative people can be any gender. You don't owe anyone anything and no one owes you anything. You also don't need to justify yourself if you don't want to date or have sex with someone; it's your choice.

# CHAPTER 17

## Train

Near Sarah's house, there was a tunnel. The tunnel went underneath the road and was probably meant to help drain water. We joked that a hobo lived in the tunnel and one day in high school, Sarah dared me to crawl through it. I *really* did not want to, but it was never easy for me to say no to Sarah. So, I crawled inside and started my journey. It was spring and inside the tunnel it was a full 10 degrees colder than outside of it. It was black, even though it was the middle of the day. To make my tunnel trip official, I had to wait until a car passed over me. This could take a while as Sarah lived in the middle of nowhere. I can't imagine this was too exciting for Sarah because she had to stand by the tunnel and wait too. I was crouched in the middle of the tunnel, praying that a car would come so I could get out. I was also praying that one wouldn't come because I did not want to be crushed. When a car did finally pass it sounded loud but muffled, and when it was over I crawled out the other side as quickly as I could.

In college, and I guess life in general, peer pressure and dares can lead you to more dangerous places than a water drainage tunnel. I did things that I am not proud of, and though peer pressure was usually involved, I am responsible for my own actions, as is everyone.

Sarah had found out about a party at an apartment in Wicker Park and she invited me. This was in January, right after we were friends again freshman year. Before the party, we pre-gamed in her dorm room and took shots of flavored vodka.

"Come on, Laurie. Shot for shot. You need to keep up."

I was abusing alcohol at this point, but I also have a weak stomach and was feeling nauseous. I ignored this and choked back shot after shot. It was getting late and I was not feeling well. I told Sarah that I did not want to go to the party anymore and she got pissed off.

"You get mad when I don't invite you to stuff and now you don't want to go? We're going."

When Sarah decided it was time for us to leave, we took two trains to the party. We still hadn't figured out the most direct route to Wicker Park and it took us forever to get there.

By the time we arrived at the party, I had started to sober up. The party was in a large apartment and we had to pay five dollars to get in. It seemed very official, with a check-in table and a woman who put our money into a cash box. We entered a huge room that was packed with people. A band was playing. The music was loud but pretty good, and people were milling about and dancing. There was a drinks table and Sarah made a beeline for it.

"I don't want to drink any more."

"I didn't invite you here to be a Debbie Downer. You at least have to hold a drink."

She handed me some jungle juice (a horrific mixture of different kinds of hard liquor and fruit juice and / or soda), stared at me wide-eyed, and nodded. I took a sip. It was sweet, but it still burned going down.

We talked and danced a bit. One glass of jungle juice turned into another and then another. When Sarah started dancing with a guy I decided to go to the bathroom. There was a long line to get in and when I got out, I couldn't find her. It was hard to understand the layout of the apartment. It was large, with many rooms that didn't serve any obvious purpose. There were just smatterings of furniture and there didn't appear to be any bedrooms. I don't think there was a kitchen either. I searched for Sarah in every room, walking in on people doing drugs and practically having sex. Drink in hand I continued searching feeling more tired and nauseous as I went. I ended up in a room that had two things in it, a desk lamp turned on the floor in the corner and a bare queen-sized mattress.

I sat down on the mattress and started to throw up. I actually feel pretty terrible about this and if it was your apartment, I'm so sorry. After a while, Sarah and her new friend found me and he told her that we had to leave. I think Sarah probably yelled at me, but I can't remember.

We walked to the train station and I assumed Sarah knew the way back to the dorm – but remember, she had been drinking too. We got onto the train and it felt good to sit down. After an indeterminate amount of time, Sarah started freaking out.

"We need to get off at the next stop. I think I spaced out and I don't know where we are."

I hadn't been paying attention to where we were either; I was too busy throwing up on the train. I take this opportunity to apologize to the person who had to clean this up too.

The next stop was Harlem. We were ridiculously far from campus and on the highway. We had practically made it to the O'Hare airport. As it was very late, trains were coming infrequently and we had to wait on the outdoor platform for ages in the cold.

At this point, I don't remember much beyond flashes of waiting at the freezing station, but I wish this had been a wake-up call. It would take me a while longer to realize that I didn't have to do the things Sarah or anyone else told me to. I am grateful that nothing bad happened to us that night or any other night that we were reckless. Many people are not so lucky.

My friend Clara couldn't understand why I was still friends with Sarah after everything she put me through, and looking back on it now, I don't understand it either.

The first time I stood up for myself to Sarah was February of my sophomore year. Sarah had gotten a fake ID during our freshman year. It's what she had used to buy us the sweet tea vodka that we got drunk on for the music festival my freshman year, but it had just been confiscated. She wanted to buy a new one and the price would be cheaper if more than one person got one with her. She wanted me to get one with her and I refused. I did not want to get in trouble with the police, I did not feel like spending the money, and really, the whole thing made me uncomfortable. She was mad about it, but I am glad I didn't get one and that I stood up to her.

If your friends or anyone else pressures you to drink or go to parties or do anything you don't want to do, get new friends. That may sound harsh, but if someone only wants to hang out with you when you do things that don't make you comfortable, you have to decide if that relationship is worth it. It's not that you don't just not owe anyone sex; you don't owe anyone your time or self-respect either.

And yes, the first time Sarah used her new fake ID, it got taken by the bouncer.

# CHAPTER 18

# Being Chased

My dad owned his hardware store for about 15 years, and in that time he went on countless business trips. We missed him, but it was pretty exciting when he would go because he always sent my sister and me a postcard. He would bring us back gifts, such as a snow globe or figurine. My sister and I made banners to welcome him home and stayed up late to see him. The best trips were when he went to fun places and could bring the whole family. These trips usually happened in October, so as an added bonus we got to miss a few days of school.

He took us to Las Vegas when I was in fifth grade and we saw this show called *Siegfried & Roy;* maybe you've heard of it. The show we saw was on October 3, 2003. When Roy was dragged off stage by Montecore, the white tiger, it seriously looked like part of the show and we sat in the audience with everyone else for probably half an hour, waiting for the show to continue.

When I was in sixth grade, we went to Orlando and got to go to Disney World and Universal Studios. Disney was as amazing as you would expect. My dad was at the hardware convention for most of the days and we often did things as a family at night. It being October, Universal was open late for something called "Halloween Horror Nights." We didn't do our research to find out what that meant; we were just excited that we could go to the park at night.

Halloween Horror Nights is a time when Universal becomes one big haunted house. Some of the rides are open late, but this comes at a price. To walk through the park, you have to walk through a corn field and get chased by men with chainsaws (or probably fake chainsaws, but in the moment, they seem real).

The night was a disaster. Only a handful of rides were running and they had lines upwards of three hours. The main attraction was a bunch of haunted houses with different themes and we were not going to go into those. With a name like "Halloween Horror Nights," I'm not too sure what we expected.

While trying to leave, we realized that most of the exits were blocked off. A man with a chainsaw was chasing my family, and my sister was *really* freaking out. Suddenly a different chainsaw man jumped out from behind a cornstalk and revved his chainsaw right next to my sister's head. She screamed and started crying.

My dad yelled at the man, "Can't you see she's just a kid? Leave her alone."

"Hey man, I'm just trying to do my job," Chainsaw man replied and walked away.

Finally we escaped, and now we reminisce and laugh about that night. I have been to Universal twice since then and it is my favorite amusement park. Harry Potter World completely exceeds the hype.

To me, when someone is chasing you or stalking you or harassing you, it was supposed to be like those men with the chainsaws – loud and insistent. That's how it was on TV shows, so it had to be that way in real life too. But when Noah started following me it was so subtle that I almost convinced myself it was a coincidence. In a school with over 15,000 undergrads alone and a city of almost three million, this was implausible but not impossible.

As I have said, wherever I went, he was there. Outside my dorm, weird places in the city, outside my classes. It took a while for the full-on harassment to start. Maybe he was afraid I would go to the police and felt he needed to silence me. I was more afraid than I had been with the chainsaw men and no one was there to yell at him and tell him I was just a kid.

I started having a recurring nightmare that I was being chased by a group of men. They all looked like Noah and they moved in slow motion. The best way I can describe the way they moved is how the creatures called The Gentlemen move in the *Buffy the Vampire Slayer* episode "Hush." In my dreams, the group of Noahs kind of float towards me slowly. No matter how fast I run, they are always right behind me. It is always night and the only light is from a lamppost. The dream is not always exactly the same, but it's close enough. I run towards a bus and I know that if I get on, I will be okay.

One time in the dream I did manage to get on the bus and then the bus driver kicked me off because my bus pass didn't work. Sometimes dreams are realistic like that. I haven't had the dream in years, but it still scares me to think about.

Dealing with Noah my freshman year, and his – following? stalking? harassment? I'm not quite sure what to call it – was terrifying. Though it wasn't easy, I do think it was a good thing that I got the Emergency Order of Protection because it made him stop. I do still wish that getting the order had been my choice. If it had been my choice, I probably would have renewed it, and my relationship with my parents wouldn't have been fractured.

It took me a while to feel safe walking around Chicago alone. Once Noah moved away, that helped tremendously.

Sometimes when someone is trying to scare you or is obsessed with you or whatever, it might not be as obvious as them chasing after you with a chainsaw. That does not mean it is any less serious and it does not mean you shouldn't get help.

# CHAPTER 19

# Getting Help

As you can probably tell, during my freshman year I fell into a fugue of partying and putting myself into dangerous situations. The worst thing that could happen had already happened and it had been my fault, so why not tempt fate? I couldn't understand how I had been raped the first time I put myself in a "dangerous situation" and that after that, even with all my partying, nothing too terrible ever happened. After about a year of this, I decided it was time to stop before I ended up killing myself. In my junior year I became a hermit, thinking that I'd used up all of my chances and my next party might be my last. Senior year, things evened out. I worked hard at school to have just under a 4.0 GPA, but still felt like a complete joke. I felt that I needed to prove to my school that I was better than that letter in my file, and I should never have been made to feel that way. I thought of my promise to myself to get the letter out of my file, but was I strong enough now and was I really innocent?

By winter break of my senior year, I was a mess. Right before going home for break, my iPhone was stolen out of my purse, and it made me feel violated all over again. Polly and I had gone to Boystown to celebrate the end of finals and the start of vacation. One second my phone was in my bag, and the next my bag was open and it was gone. More importantly though,

I was running out of time to clear my name and once I graduated I wouldn't be able to do anything about it. I know this might not make sense because, once I graduated, that paper in my file would mean literally nothing, but I needed my legacy at my school to be Summa Cum Laude, not Liar Laurie. One of these things would happen.

Around this time, Title IX lawsuits were happening at universities around the country. I would read about these cases while my family buried themselves in holiday preparations. Title IX of the Education Amendments Act of 1972 is supposed to ensure that all students at a school are able to have equal access to education. If there is a hostile environment, like rape or harassment, the school has to take action to protect the complainant or lose their federal funding. This is why schools have judicial cases and hearing committees where they find a student responsible or not. Retaliation from the school is also strictly prohibited – something that the Vice President of Student Affairs must have known, but ignored.

I had never heard of Title IX lawsuits before, but out of nowhere these cases were everywhere. People were taking out lawsuits against their schools for butchering their cases and getting real results. I thought about doing a case against my school and this seemed like a chance for some type of justice, but just as this idea became a possibility, I discovered that the statute of limitations for my case had run out. I celebrated Christmas and Hanukkah while trying to come to terms with the fact that there may never be any justice for Liar Laurie.

As part of my degree, I was able to take one elective. That's right – for four years and 12 terms I got exactly one class that could be anything. I had saved this for my term before student teaching (my school has three terms each school year). I was going to take creative writing. When I started taking this class in January of my senior year, I was completely out of my element. The simplest assignments took me hours and I felt like I was the worst writer in the class. I hadn't written a fictional story since elementary school, and even then I was never very good. For whatever reason, though, the class sounded fun enough to be worthy of my one elective.

A theme started emerging in my poems and writing assignments. I couldn't stop writing about girls who had horrible things happen to them. Sometimes I wrote from the point of view of a bystander, sometimes from that of the girl – or even the perpetrator. Here is the first poem I wrote for my class. No, I did not turn it in.

### I'm a Liar and a Tease

Kissed him
Took off my shirt
Didn't go to the police
But you told me not to
Told me not to waste their time
Told me let the school handle it

Nothing

Now tell me that I made it up
That it never went any further that ...

Second Saturday
Smashed
New city, no friends
Smashed
1453
Smashed
Blackout in a can

Can't stand it
That I took your offer to lie down on your bed
Smashed
My head against the headboard

Laugh, lay into me

Your handprint hot on my cheek
It's cold with the open window
Capitulate, deescalate, cap off

Breath like sweet orange juice
Haze of soft light
Eyes, brown, but like amber
Sun rising when you let me go
Branded: bite marks and bruises, I'm a liar and a tease

My main problem with this poem is that it says "second Saturday", but I can't ignore a good ol' alliteration! I told myself that this was okay, because for most students it was the second Saturday. It was the third for me because of freshman orientation. Another awkward thing about this poem is the "sweet orange juice" part. I told him that his breath smelled, so he drank some orange juice. No joke. People of Earth, if someone tells you that your breath smells, don't think orange juice will fix this! Also, don't rape. Orange juice did not make his breath smell "sweet," it probably made it worse. This whole interaction happened when he seemed somewhat normal and I was lucid enough to notice such things.

This poem makes me feel angry or something. I guess it's a bit punchy, like I'm punching something with my words. I know, pretentious. I was very angry when I wrote it and maybe it helped me get some of that out. I got a bit Thesaurus.com happy, but this happens to the best of us and Noah probably didn't have a headboard, he smashed my head into the wall. The name of this file on my computer is actually "Waiting Room Poem." It's all of the things that raced through my head when I waited for my hearing.

For our final assignment in creative writing, we had to write a short story, and I started writing a story about a boy named Ben. Ben goes out onto the lake by his house and when he comes home he finds his house empty, but not the same. He goes to his room and discovers that his brother, Kirk, who died before he was born, never died in this different reality, meaning Ben does not exist there. Ben meets up with his best friend, Anna, in his reality. In this reality she doesn't know him. They talk and he learns the devastating truth. His brother, Kirk, raped her. At that point I was like … wow. I tried to write a sci-fi story – I really tried – and even that had to have rape in it.

I realized then that I would never be able to write anything else until I wrote out my story. Two years later and I am still having this same problem. So, I set about writing out the story of that night. It took me about a month to write it all out and I don't think I'll ever be one hundred percent happy with it. I changed my best friend's name to Sarah, as I have done here, and I started the story in the playground where we went after the party. I named the main character Lindy because it would be important for her to have an "L" name, to be "Liar Lindy." We see Lindy in the playground, drunk on the swing, feeling giddy and just trying to fit in and have a good time. I explained how Sarah had been sent the vacuum and how they had been drinking Four Lokos. Originally the story was meant to center around the hearing against me and the night of the rape would be a flashback in the waiting room, but I quickly realized that this was going to make the story way too long and lose its focus.

Lindy and I are actually pretty different from each other. Lindy has red hair and my hair is blonde, except for in certain lights when it looks red … maybe we're not that different. I wrote that Lindy was wearing a pink tank top that night, because it was important to me, at the time, that she wear a strapless bra. Not just any strapless bra, but the one she bought for prom. Hers was black and mine was nude. See? Different! I didn't think it was worth it to explain that she wore a Free People top with sleeves that just showed her bra straps, so a strapless bra would be needed. A pink tank top was a weird mix of that night and my prom dress. Lindy has a slight sunburn; I wear sunscreen 365. I wrote out every detail of that night that I could remember, and in writing it out I felt such gratitude to my past self and everything I endured to survive. Seeing my story in black and white on the computer screen, my feelings of responsibility for what happened began to lessen.

The story I wrote is probably best described as creative nonfiction. I wrote about the rape in detail (or the details I could remember), and this felt okay, because it was Lindy being raped, not me. She willingly goes into Noah's bedroom and passes out. She wakes up to Noah kissing her and she even says, "You can take my bra off if you want to." She loses her virginity in the most horrific way imaginable and leaves the apartment alone, as the sun is rising. It's hard for me to read this story and know that all those things did not just happen to Lindy – they also happened to me.

Writing the rape part of the story wasn't easy. I wrote earlier versions that glossed over what happened and other versions that were more graphic. I guess what I turned in is somewhere in the middle.

Lindy kills herself at the end of the story and at the time it felt safe that she was dead. Dead, she was protected and she would never end up in that waiting room. Lindy never goes to the Dean and never has a case against her. Her death is detailed, but I needed it to feel real.

Writing that story was the first step in my healing. I turned my story in to class and thought that was that. I thought I was clever changing names and details. *No one will ever figure out that Lindy is me!*

I have chosen to include the story that I wrote for my creative writing class here. Please remember it is a piece of creative nonfiction, or at least that's what it most closely resembles. It is as close to what happened to me as I can remember, but it is not an account of what happened. You may notice that some details have been changed, but the truth of the story is the same. I did not feel that I could tell *my* story without including this one, as writing it was the catalyst for my healing. I do describe being raped and Lindy's suicide, so if this may be triggering for you, please skip this part and I'll see you in the next chapter. No hard feelings.

## We Can't Fly

*Lindy let go of the chains and felt that the curved plastic seat beneath her was wobbling back and forth. When she swung forward, she quickly grabbed onto them to keep herself from falling off. Her eyes were closed and she could hear the swoosh of cars speeding towards their destinations now mixed with the clicking freewheel of a biker. As she moved up and down her long red hair would become airborne for a moment and then crash into her back. The wind moved past her and she could feel that the air had changed. What had been a hot Chicago September day was now a cold Chicago September night. Letting go of the chains again the seat rocked forcing her to lean back, her hair now dragging on the ground beneath her as she grabbed the chains just in time.*

*"Jesus, Lindy, don't do that," Steven yelled from the picnic table. "We need to get out of here," he yelled, addressing the rest of the group. "I'm sick of playing babysitter."*

*They were in the Parker Elementary School playground, right off the university's campus. When they had first arrived Lindy and Sarah had peed behind a slide. Lindy had been apprehensive; wouldn't someone see them? But the boys had promised to look away and Sarah assured her it was dark out and the street lamps' glow didn't reach this part of the playground.*

*"We can't take her back to the dorm. She's way too drunk. We'll all get in trouble," Paul said as he jumped off the monkey bars.*

*"I'm not too drunk. I'm not even drrrrrruunnnk," Lindy said through giggles.*

*"Lindy, darling, please get off the swings. I don't want you to kill yourself or someone else," Sarah shouted from a horse spring rider.*

*"I can't, I don't want to go. Don't make me go, Sarah," Lindy slurred.*

*Lindy was feeling that feeling she had discovered the first time she had been drunk. This had been the previous weekend at a house party with Sarah. After a few beers she had unexpectedly felt giddy and invincible.*

"Well, some of us want to get out of here," Steven responded.

"Shit, how much did she have to drink?" Paul asked.

"Like two Four Lokos, maybe more," Sarah told him.

Lindy was trying to not let it bother her that neither Paul nor Steven had paid her any attention all night. They were really her roommate Sarah's friends from high school and if anything, they had both been busy flirting with Sarah. At the party they had just come from, the three of them had disappeared into the crowd and Lindy had found herself alone on a staircase drinking a grape flavored Four Loko. It was her first time having one and the taste had been sweet and sickening. After the grape she had moved on to watermelon which had succeeded in being even more disgusting. By the time the police showed up and they ran from the party, Lindy was unsure about how much she had had to drink. They had then come to the playground to regroup and figure out where to go next.

"Well, I don't feel like staying in a playground all night. It's fucking cold now and it's only 2.15," Steven said irritably while looking at his phone.

"Oh, I know! We can go to 1453. I know a guy that lives there," Sarah responded.

"Sarah, I need to pee. Like soooo bad," Lindy slurred.

"Okay. Don't worry. We're going to 1453. I just texted Tony."

On Monday, Sarah's mother had sent her a vacuum in the mail and Lindy had helped her lug it across campus from the mail center to their dorm, Corval Hall. It had been a sunny day that belonged in July and they both were quickly covered in sweat. Lindy didn't think having a vacuumed dorm was worth this. When they were about to give up, Tony had come along. He was a senior and had been wearing a tight white t-shirt which showed off his sculpted chest and arms. He had carried the vacuum the rest of the way to the dorm and even up the four flights of stairs to their room. Sarah had asked for his number and when he revealed he lived in 1453 they couldn't believe their luck.

When they arrived at 1453, Tony was standing outside the

*building smoking a cigarette. He greeted them, took a final drag, and put it out on the sidewalk. The group then entered the building and made quick work of signing in.*

*"Do you like 1453?" Sarah asked Tony in the elevator.*

*"Fuck yeah, no rules like in the dorms. I mean it's like you get the benefits of a dorm with laundry and security and activities and shit, but no RA breathing down your throat. I've already had like four parties since school started."*

*Sarah grinned at Lindy. Yes, this was the place they were supposed to be.*

*When they got inside the apartment Lindy announced, "I really need to pee."*

*"Yeah bathroom's the first door on the left," Tony told her.*

*Lindy was learning that alcohol made you have to pee. A lot. As she sat on the toilet it occurred to her that her eyes were closed and her head was in her lap. She had no idea how long she had been like this. She got up and washed her hands, almost falling over as she stood up. In the mirror above the sink, her eyes looked red. She gave her hair a few shakes and tried to remember how she had managed to get dirt and wood chips in it. Her dark eye make-up was smeared under her eyes and extended down her left cheek. Sarah had so carefully given her a smoky eye earlier that night and now it was wrecked. Lindy quickly grabbed some toilet paper and wet it to wipe away the mess, which worked too well. She stopped when she realized she was taking off her foundation too, revealing her sunburnt pink skin. Her teeth felt numb, an unfortunate side effect to finally drinking. She cupped her hands to drink some water which relieved her dry throat but unsettled her stomach. Lindy patted her face dry and felt her stomach move again. She grabbed the sink and leaned forward, closing her eyes. The nausea passed as she told herself, "Lindy Bishop, you will not throw up. Do not fuck this up." She gave her reflection a smile and exited the bathroom.*

*Lindy could hear voices around the corner and walked towards them. Everyone was in a small living room with a large window. Across the street Lindy could see apartment buildings with most of* their windows dark. She wondered, were the people who lived there asleep or still out?

Steven and Paul sat on orange plastic chairs and Tony had his arm around Sarah on a futon covered in fake white leather. They each had a half-empty glass of brown liquid on the coffee table in front of them. There was a full glass next to Sarah's and Lindy wondered if it was meant for her. The room was brightly lit and this startled her. She was swaying on her feet. All she wanted was to sit down, but all of the seats were taken. Sarah looked up when she entered the room and picked up the drink.

"Lindy, oh my gosh I was about to come check on you. You were in there for like 15 minutes. Here, I made you a drink, rum and Coke."

Sarah handed Lindy the drink, now lukewarm. Lindy was afraid she would throw up if she drank any more, but she also didn't want to look lame in front of her new friends.

"Don't worry, it's Diet," Sarah told her.

Lindy took a sip. It tasted like Coke, but wrong. It went down harsher than a Four Loko. She felt tired and her legs didn't want to hold her up any longer. She thought about sitting on the floor, but how stupid would that look? Instead Lindy crossed the room to the opposite wall and decided to lean on it. She stared at the large TV mounted on the other wall, silently showing an infomercial for some workout DVDs. Dubstep played in a steady stream. Lindy felt the vibrations of the bass drops as her head pounded. The conversation continued, but Lindy could never quite pick up what they were talking about. She just wanted to go back to the dorm and sleep.

"Whoa looks like you're about to drop that."

In front of Lindy stood a man who looked like he was in his twenties, definitely older than her. He was wearing a grey t-shirt with the NFL logo on it and he was tall. Lindy's standard for how tall a guy should be came from her father, who was 6 feet. This guy was taller and the sun agreed with him. His dusky hair stood out against his tan skin and brown eyes. He took the drink out of her hand and placed it on the floor.

*"Hi. I'm Noah."*

*Lindy stared at him.*

*"And you have a name, right?"*

*Lindy giggled and smiled.*

*"I'm Lindy. I'm a friend of Tony's."*

*"I'm Tony's roommate. I figured I'd come out and see what was going on. He's always having people over. Imagine my surprise when I see this cute little redhead right outside my bedroom door."*

*Lindy giggled again and felt her cheeks getting warm. Even while leaning on the wall she continued to sway, but here was this guy – this really cute guy – and he was talking to her, Lindy.*

*"So, you go to Holbrook?" he asked her.*

*"Yeah, well at least for the past two weeks anyway."*

*"Me too. Jeez, it's already been two weeks?"*

*"I guess it is going pretty fast. So, you're a freshman too?"*

*He didn't look like a freshman.*

*"Not exactly, but it's my first year at Holbrook."*

*Lindy swayed and Noah put his hand on her shoulder.*

*"Whoa there. Do you want to lay down?" he asked her.*

*"Um, yes, thank you." Lindy had never felt so grateful.*

*Noah opened the door to his bedroom and motioned for Lindy to come inside. He turned on the small lamp on his bedside table and the room was illuminated in its dim glow. Noah closed the door, muffling the music and voices in the living room. The window on the far wall was open and the room was filled with the faint sound of cars passing five stories below. In her pink tank top Lindy shivered. Noah's bed was pushed against the wall in the corner. It was a twin and it took up most of the space. The room was not much bigger than the walk-in closet she shared with Sarah at their dorm.*

*Lindy sat down on the edge of his bed and took off her sandals. Her feet were freezing. A clock on Noah's desk by the window told her it was 3:41. Next to the clock were three textbooks in a neat pile and a Mac desktop computer. In a framed photo Noah was sitting* on the steps of a Spanish style house with another boy who looked like him but younger. A brother, maybe? Each boy was smiling in a colorful Ralph Lauren Polo, with one hand on a panting Doberman.

Lindy lay back on top of his covers, wanting to get under them for warmth, but didn't feel like she should. She breathed in and smelled the scent of clean laundry. It made her think of when she had tried to make her mom perfume for her birthday out of watered down laundry detergent, but this was back in a time when people still called her Linda.

"Comfy?" Noah asked as he lay down beside her.

Lindy could barely hear him.

"Mmm hmmm," was all she could manage as she passed out.

When Lindy felt Noah's lips on hers, it surprised her. She opened her eyes and instinctively kissed him back. She was disoriented as to how long she had been asleep, but she could see that the lamp was on and it was still dark out. He was now on top of her and she breathed in deeply. He smelled like soap. Noah put his hands into her hair and started kissing her more forcefully, pushing his tongue into her mouth. He tasted like the cigarette she had tried the weekend before and she wondered if you could get second-hand smoke from kissing someone. She tentatively put her hands into his hair. It was soft and short; she liked the way it felt. As they kissed, Lindy could feel herself getting wet, a feeling that always embarrassed her. She felt his hands at the hem of her shirt, pulling it over her head. Her head felt hazy as she was left in the black strapless bra she had purchased for senior prom.

"You can take my bra off if you want to."

The words came out and Lindy didn't know where they had come from. She bit her lower lip as she lifted her torso and felt Noah's hands leave her hair and reemerge at her chest. Noah put his hands under her back and unhooked her bra. He threw it on the floor and started kneading her breasts. He leaned forward and took her right nipple into his mouth, biting hard.

"Ow, that hurts."

*Noah repeated the action with her other nipple.*

*Lindy tried to push him off of her.*

*"I said that hurts."*

*"But Lindy, you told me to take your bra off."*

*Lindy felt the cold air on her exposed skin. Her nipples were throbbing from where he'd bitten her. She now understood it was time to be afraid.*

*"I want to go. My friends are probably wondering what happened to me."*

*"Your friends? When you were sleeping they left with Tony to go pick up."*

*Lindy didn't know what it meant to "pick up," but she couldn't believe they would leave her, especially Sarah.*

*"Sarah," she called out, but got no response.*

*"I told you no one else is here."*

*Lindy now noticed that the hum of music was gone. No voices dropping and rising in conversation. The silence was only cut by Lindy and Noah's heavy breathing and the cars rushing past the building down below.*

*"Well it's late. I need to go."*

*Lindy sat up covering her breasts with her arm. Noah pushed her back down with both hands and then moved them to the waistband of her jeans and started to unbutton them.*

*"Stop. I don't want to go any further."*

*Lindy tried to sit up again. She was breathing fast, short breaths and her heart rate was picking up. He didn't need to push her back down this time. Her body didn't want to cooperate. Her head was throbbing and she felt heavy.*

*Noah kneeled in between her legs and pulled her jeans and panties down. She started kicking him and he leaned forward and slapped her, making her cry out. He continued until all of her clothing was on the floor and he was still fully dressed. Lindy felt the cool air trace every inch of her skin. Noah slipped a warm finger into her core as she cried.*

"Stop, please don't touch me there."

"Coming off like you don't want this when you're this fucking wet."

He removed his finger and showed Lindy the evidence of her previous arousal.

"Please stop," she cried. "Please just let me go."

Noah pulled down his sweat pants and boxers. He started rubbing himself and leaned over Lindy to grab a condom from his bedside table. The sound of the packaging opening and of him putting it on himself made her heart start racing. He pushed her legs apart and kneeled in between them, pressing into her thighs and bruising her pale skin. Lindy cried harder, not truly believing what was about to happen to her.

Noah put his hand over her mouth as she lost something she'd always imagined giving. Lindy screamed in pain, the sound barely muffled. She pushed against his chest, just wanting the agony to stop. She started struggling harder, trying to close her legs and push him off of her. Noah grabbed her by her shoulders and pulled her forward hard and back again, her head smashing into the wall behind her. Lindy's vision blackened and she couldn't see Noah on top of her, the open window, or the dim lighting. All she could hear was her own heartbeat and a constant ringing. She closed her eyes and when she opened them she scanned the room but everything seemed to have soft edges that bled into each other like a picture taken out of focus. The smell of clean laundry and soap surrounded her, mixed with sweat and cigarettes. She could see Noah's desk across the room, covered in strange shadows. It seemed to expand and contract, like a heart pulsating. From his clock a blue glow of distorted numbers twisted into the air as tendrils of light reached out to her.

Noah had his hands on her arms, squeezing them. He was grunting and groaning, going faster now. Every thrust created more stabbing pain.

"Fuck I'm close."

He stilled inside of her and his mouth went back to her right nipple, biting harder than before.

*Her vision became clearer with the jolt of pain and she looked up at him. She had been wrong before; his eyes weren't brown. They were more orange, almost like amber.*

*The next summer Lindy would lock herself in her bathroom while her parents slept. A thousand miles away Noah would be brushing his teeth, getting ready for another night of sleep and a new day tomorrow. Lindy would sit on the cold tile floor, choking back vodka as she swallowed pill after pill. She would lay down for the last time and stare up at the white glow of the light on the ceiling. The whir of the fan that automatically came on with the light would comfort her as she imagined what her life would have been like if she hadn't told Noah he could take her bra off, if she hadn't been so drunk and gone into his bedroom, if she had run just a little bit slower and been arrested at the party, if she hadn't accepted the help from Tony to carry the vacuum.*

*But for now Noah pulled out of her, saying, "You should really go. I need to get some sleep."*

*Lindy couldn't stop shaking as she put on her clothes. She exited the building and walked towards her dorm, trying to ignore the burning pain in between her legs. She made it two blocks before she vomited on the sidewalk. She cried when she realized some of it had gotten into her hair. Lindy looked up and saw that the sky was lightening. Pink clouds glowed against an amber sky, like cotton candy on fire.*

# CHAPTER 20

# Letting it Out

It was the day of my creative writing class when we would be discussing my story. It was a hybrid class; we had online assignments due on Tuesdays and met in person on Thursdays. Well, actually, we were supposed to have discussed my story the previous week. Professor Palmer had emailed asking for volunteers to have their stories workshopped first. Our stories were to be posted to our online message board and everyone was to read each other's stories and write them some comments. Then we were going to workshop each other's stories in class.

I had volunteered to go first. I had a lot of anxiety surrounding my story and I knew that the sooner it was read and discussed the better. On the day that we were to discuss my story, we had spent part of the class discussing a short story we had read for homework, and then when it came to workshop time we discussed the story of one of my classmates. He had apparently volunteered too. Through the class, I kept glancing at the clock to see if there would be any time to discuss my story. Class ended and I was anxious that I would have to wait a week to have my story discussed. I was afraid of what people would say. Would they think that Lindy consented? Had she not fought enough? Would they laugh at the fact that she willingly went into his bedroom? And she told him he could take her bra off; surely someone would fault her for that.

When our next class rolled around, I sat down at my usual spot in the right back corner of the room and spread out my materials for class: folder, notebook, pencil case, and my journal that we were required to write in. No one sat next to me on either side, but this didn't bother me. The class was small, maybe 15 people. The people were fine, I just didn't have it in me to invest in relationships with them. There was one guy in the class who emailed me a lot with questions on the homework, but never spoke to me in class. That's weird, right?

The people in the class were mostly freshmen and sophomores – this was an introductory writing class. That day, with my things spread around me, I felt protected. I looked at the clock in the back of the room and saw that class should have started a minute earlier. No one spoke to each other and I started thinking it was a little strange for the professor to be late, but not unheard of. Not that one minute is terribly late, but he was usually early. I was also anxious about class that day, so a minute felt like eternity. Everyone sat in a semi-circle formation, so you could see everyone in the class. I looked around at my peers for a moment, but then cast my eyes down. I didn't want to make eye contact. I already felt too vulnerable. The door opened and Professor Palmer came in. He stood by the door and we all turned to look at him. He looked determined and out of breath.

"Laurie, can I speak to you?"

I probably said, "Sure", or something like that.

I got up from my seat and followed him outside. In the hall, a group of students were sitting on some armchairs, studying. I stopped right outside the room, feeling defiant and trying to show that I did not care who heard what he had to say to me. In actuality, I was mortified.

"Here, let's come over here." He motioned for me to move down the hall. After a few steps I stopped, still not wanting to show that I cared.

"I just want to make sure you're okay to have your story discussed. It's a workshop, so I can't control what people are going to say."

I looked away and made myself smile. "Yeah. It's okay."

"It's okay?"

"It's okay."

"Okay then."

We walked back into the classroom and I sat down with my heart racing. Had he guessed that Lindy was me? I had changed the names of buildings and streets, but it might have still been obvious. The real address of Noah's building was changed to 1453! There was no way anyone could tell the story took place at my school. I was worried that if he had figured it out then people in the class might have figured it out too, but I still didn't know for sure what he thought he knew.

We spent most of the class discussing my story. Longer than anyone else's. The first thing I had to do was to read a passage from my story aloud to the class, and I chose to read the part where Lindy is drunk in the bathroom right after arriving at Noah and Tony's apartment. I used Tony's real name in my story and I'm not sure why, but here he gets to be "Tony". It's kind of funny because I was super proud of that part in the bathroom, and when I got my edited draft back from Professor Palmer at the end of class, that was the part of the story that he had edited the most, with tons of what I will call "constructive criticism".

After I finished reading that scene, it was time for feedback. I took a deep breath and looked up from my story to face my peers. This was the moment – all it would take was one person saying that it was her fault. My professor was sitting there thinking whatever he thought, and I felt exposed. It was probably awkward for him to lead the discussion, but he didn't show this.

"So, can someone summarize the story for us?"

A girl who I had never spoken to raised her hand. "There's a girl named Lindy and she gets drunk. She goes to a guy's apartment and her friends leave her and she consents to kissing this guy and being in his bed, but then he rapes her. In the end she commits suicide."

A boy in the class raised his hand next. "Yeah, I wasn't sure where the story was going. There was lot of rising action and I wasn't sure how Noah fit into the story, but I kind of like that we don't meet him until the end. And yeah, it's pretty clear he rapes her."

Another girl chimed in, "She went out with her friends and she wasn't looking to do anything bad. She seems kind of naive and she's never had sex. I think that detail is important to understand her character and how much this affects her."

A boy who participated a lot said, "I like the detail about him tasting like cigarettes and her thoughts around this. It just shows how young and naive she was. And Noah is more developed than I thought he would be."

Others in the class nodded in agreement. He continued, "He really seems like a real person. And that makes it more painful, like he has a dog."

I was relieved that they noticed this. It was important to me that Noah be a developed character, because the real Noah is a real person. A real person with hopes and fears and a dog. A real person who forced his penis into my vagina. That's just reality.

I felt stronger and like I could take ownership of this story. I also felt proud of myself hearing my peers comment on the writing itself and the content. Everyone said she was raped. I felt I needed an outside source to confirm this and they did. I answered my peers' questions, like why did I name it *We Can't Fly?* The answer I gave was to show what people can and cannot handle, and what is not possible for a human to do and what can break them. People can't fly and maybe being raped and surviving after this is equally impossible. Maybe that's a little too hard to follow, but that's how I came up with it. This is also not even remotely true, but at the time I was actively suicidal and that's how I felt.

As the class went on, I heard my classmates continue to express their compassion for Lindy and that it was not her fault. The relief I felt was staggering. No one said anything cruel and no one blamed her. To them, she clearly hadn't consented and had been raped. The only thing that bothered me was that my classmates and my professor questioned if Lindy had to die. I had created Lindy, and if she was going to die, it was my choice.

At the end of class, my peers handed me their written comments, and to this day the comments still touch me. Part of the criteria for a comment was that you had to summarize the story and then give feedback. I got kind feedback and no one had anything negative to say. In everyone's summary, Lindy was a good person who was let down by her friends and raped. One peer even wrote about the second-to-last paragraph, when she is trying to figure out what she did to cause this to happen to her, but that it was no one's fault but Noah's. Another peer said they thought that based on title and the opening scene that the story would be about Lindy jumping off the swings and getting injured, but that what really happens is much worse. I don't know why, but the thought of that being the story just made me laugh. Some people just don't get the title, and I guess it's no longer appropriate.

After class, I asked to speak with my professor because I was a little freaked out. I really had to go to the bathroom and he said to meet him in his office. I went to the bathroom and then went about finding his office suite, which he said was on the same floor as our class. I saw a sign for the English professor offices, leading down a hallway. I followed it to a door that you needed a passcode to open. I needed to talk to him and I wasn't sure how to get in. Being the resourceful person that I am, I opened my creative writing folder and found the class syllabus with his office number on it. I called his number and left a beautiful message that was something like this.

"Hi, it's Laurie. Laurie Katz from your creative writing class. I'm outside your office and I don't know the code, so I can't get in. So, um, I'm going to wait five minutes and then I'm going to go."

If I could not talk to him then I would have to wait a whole week, and I needed to talk to him. About two minutes later, he emerged and said, "Come with me." We walked around the corner and there was this huge office suite with windows looking in and a secretary. I had never noticed this giant office suite in all my times of going to class. I guess I was super focused every Thursday and never turned my head in that direction. I was pretty embarrassed, but it made the whole, "I'm talking to you because I think you think I was raped and that's a little awkward / accurate," thing less awkward.

As we walked through the suite to his office, he asked me what my major was, and I told him I was studying early childhood education. For those few moments it made me feel better to talk about normal things. When we got to his office, another girl from the class was waiting to talk to him and she said I could go first. I most certainly did not want to go first and have her waiting through our conversation. I told her she could go and after a bit more back and forth, she did. So, I waited some more and thought of what I would say. I thought about leaving, but knew that this was what I needed to do and where I needed to be.

Eventually the girl left and I entered his office and took a seat. I had put my winter coat on and this helped me feel protected, but also made me overheated. I didn't know what to say. I'd rehearsed some things in the hall, but I couldn't remember them now. As I sat in the uncomfortable silence I could feel him looking at me, and it occurred to me that I might be in trouble. This was a creative writing class for fiction. What I had written wasn't exactly fiction. The first thing I managed to say was, "I didn't mean to cheat, or anything like that."

With that I outed myself and I felt my heart pounding.

"No, I never thought that," Professor Palmer said while shaking his head.

That was all it took. I can't remember whether I cried or not. Knowing me I probably did. I told him everything that had happened. The rape. The case. Court. The case against me. Everything. I'd never told anyone the whole thing and it poured out of me. I didn't go into details about anything too deeply, I just gave him the timeline. I told him the things said to me by the Vice President of Student Affairs that stuck out like, "Liar Laurie," and "extremely emotional for him and his family." He listened the entire time and it felt so good to be heard. He didn't doubt what I told him. No, he believed me.

"I'm so sorry for what you went through," he told me. A large factor in someone's healing process is the reactions of others, and this was the first time I had a truly helpful reaction. Between my words and his and the class discussion, my pain suddenly felt valid. I'm going to say at this point I was most definitely crying.

"You're not going to do anything like Lindy does at the end of your story, right?" he asked me.

"No, I wouldn't do that, I already ..."

"You already, what?"

"The summer after my freshman year was really hard. And, well, I'm glad it didn't work."

"I'm glad it didn't work too."

In actuality, I still struggled every day not to kill myself, and I told myself that I could either go to class or go through with it. The pain I had buried for almost four years overtook me that winter. But I wasn't going to tell him that. I did not need another terrible encounter in the counseling center – more on that later.

Professor Palmer wanted to help in any way he could, and I expressed my desire to get the letter removed from my file. The next day, by coincidence, the English department had a meeting about sexual assault planned and he would see what information he could get. So, I left his office feeling better than I had in long while. He emailed me that weekend to see that I was more or less okay, and I responded that I wasn't "planning anything stupid." And for the first time in a long time, I meant it.

I went back to my apartment and read his feedback on my story. I cried as I read it and wondered if he had realized it was real before or after writing his comments. He saw that Lindy was raped and recognized the painful details. I had carried this in silence and suddenly I had a voice. Not just through Lindy, but through me.

The next week after class, my professor asked to speak with me and we went back to his office. I was kind of surprised. I figured he probably felt he had done enough and I didn't expect him to bring it up again. When I sat down, I felt much more comfortable this time. I even left my coat off. At the meeting with his department, he had learned that it had just been decided that when a student disclosed an assault to a professor, they would have to tell the Dean. Again, this was 2015 and things were just starting to be done to make colleges accountable for rapes on campus. Even so, I felt betrayed and the thought of the Dean brought back my memories of how he hurt and manipulated me. Professor Palmer explained that he had spoken to the Dean on the phone and it was a new dean – a woman.

The Dean of Students was now a woman and I had not even realized it. That night, when I looked up the Dean from my freshman year, I saw that he had been gone for almost a whole year. I also saw that the Vice President of Student Affairs had left the school too. Even the woman who had called me and told me not to go to the police had left. Sarah was out of my life and Noah was long gone, so that just left me. I was the only person left and I was carrying the weight of everything that had happened alone.

My professor said that the new Dean had told him that there were things about my case that he didn't know about. I feel like she said this to make him doubt what I had told him, and I started to feel more betrayal from my school. The big message of their phone call had been that, without new information, it was highly unlikely anything could be changed.

I told him, "It's okay. It wasn't the answer I was hoping for, but it's okay."

I didn't believe it was okay, but by saying it was, maybe I could convince myself.

"I'll go with you if you still want to meet with her."

I was grateful for the offer, but I had my answer. I couldn't fight something that couldn't be changed and meeting with her wouldn't have done anything. I cried, like a lot, and had to let go of my promise to myself. I felt a little awkward crying that hard in front of him, being the ugly crier that I am. But once I started I couldn't stop. After I had composed myself I left his office, questioning what I would do now that changing my file wasn't an option.

As part of the class and as the point of the workshops, we had to revise our stories. This was not easy for me. The changes I made probably made it a better story, but it was hard to take the story further away from what really happened. Sometimes the truth isn't as eloquent as fiction. I revised my story because I was committed to the grade, but I don't feel much affinity towards the revised version. It was also a little awkward turning in my revised story and getting feedback, knowing my professor knew the story was based on something that happened, but he was very professional about the whole thing. I have reread my story maybe twice since I graduated and I always read the first draft.

Professor Palmer and I met two or three more times after class. I think he wanted to make sure I was really okay. I was also curious about how he had figured out the story was based on something that had happened.

"I really don't know," he told me. "I read a lot of student work and I just knew that your story was real."

This wasn't a very satisfying answer. I wanted to know what had given me away, but I could not be more grateful that he saw some moment in my writing that put it together for him.

One day after class he asked if I had been able to have any relationships, and all I could do was shake my head. I thought of Tristan, but that wasn't really a relationship and I would never be with someone like that again. I couldn't stand to be touched, and even hugs made me panic. I was afraid that I would never feel safe enough to be with someone.

He was also adamant that I find a therapist. Every time I saw him, he asked if I had found one. I was resistant to this idea and told him as much.

"I know that you can get through this, but therapy will help you get there faster." He told me about a struggle in his own life and how therapy had been helpful for him. This is what made me decide that I would do it. I researched therapists in Chicago and found Kelly. She specialized in helping people who had been through sexual trauma and she looked kind in her photo. I had my first session two days before my creative writing class ended and I told Professor Palmer that I had an appointment. He seemed genuinely happy that I was getting help and urged me to stick with it.

The last time I saw him was after I had been student teaching for a couple weeks. I met with him to get my final portfolio back. No way did I want that floating around my school. It felt strange to see him and I felt a little awkward about all that I had shared, but he was as kind as ever.

I am so grateful for all that he did for me and I can never repay him. I might have actually committed suicide if I hadn't gotten help when I did. I still email him occasionally and I am always sure to thank him. It's nice to check in and to express my gratitude.

# CHAPTER 21

## Therapy

This wasn't the first time I had tried therapy. The summer after my freshman year, I decided to see a therapist. I had toyed with therapy before, but I was afraid to face my problems. I went to see a therapist at my school's counseling center soon after that September night. I went because, in a moment of desperation, I had told one of my professors a little of what was going on.

On my way to her class, I had seen Noah for the first time since that night and had felt panicked and terrified through her class. She had tried to be helpful, but ended up telling another professor what had happened without my permission. The two of them had then dragged me to the counseling center

This professor meant well and even went with me to one of my meetings with the Dean, but she tried to take over and tell me what I needed to do and I just couldn't have that.

The therapist at the counseling center had been pushy, and it was at a time when I wasn't ready to admit to her or myself what had happened. So I went the one time I was forced to go and canceled my second appointment. Late one night, while I was waiting to hear back about the case against me, I called the on-call emergency counselor through my school, but was more interested in why I would not tell him my name than in what happened to me.

That summer after my freshman year, when I saw a therapist in Boston, it was a disaster. She seemed nice at first and I told her what had happened and the case against me. Her response was to ask me, "Are you still drinking?"

"Are you still drinking?" translates to "You were raped because you were drunk." I don't think I need to explain why that was triggering. Her question pushed me to a dark place and I am so grateful that it did not work and I am still here today.

In my sophomore year, I continued to struggle and, in an attempt to get help, I told one of my professors that I was having suicidal thoughts. I was so nervous to do it, but I pushed myself to talk to him because I was desperate. He had told the class how he had struggled with suicidal thoughts through his teens and early twenties, so I thought he would "get it" and really help me. But I think he didn't know what to do with this information and really, I guess I can't blame him. I just wanted to tell someone what had happened and for them to listen. I felt I could trust him; he had always been so helpful. I needed someone I trusted to care about the rape and help me get help. I was so alone and so afraid that I would actually kill myself.

He refused to talk to me.

He just sent me back to the counseling center, and this time it was worse. The woman I met with said, "I see here how you met with the Dean of Students and there were a few hearings you were involved with." Wow. These people must really have wanted me to drop out or actually die. To share my case with the counseling center was beyond cruel and beyond unethical. I couldn't get help there, so I told her that what I said to my professor was a misunderstanding, and I just continued to use alcohol and other dangerous things as my coping mechanisms. After that, my trust in people plummeted further, and I gave up on trying to get help.

I told Professor Palmer about what had happened at the counseling center (not how I ended up there) and he said that when he spoke to the new Dean, she said this wasn't possible.

This really bothered me. *You already had me down as a liar for something much bigger, so why pretend that this didn't happen?* I also tried seeing a different therapist sophomore year, but we just didn't click and it didn't help.

I had also been cutting myself off and on through the years as a way to cope, and my reliance on this at times had been frightening. I had first started cutting myself in middle school (motivated by school pressure, bullying, and depression), but I hadn't done it in about five years by the time I went to college. Cutting gave a distinct focus to my pain, and for a few moments I didn't feel the intense pressure in my chest and I wasn't overcome with distressing emotions. I could breathe. And though the moments came at a cost, inflicting physical pain was an easy choice compared to what I was going through internally. Somehow, near the end of my sophomore year, I got myself not just to stop partying so much, but also to pull back on how often I was cutting. After that time, in a way I felt more defeated and emptier than ever. I had lost my ways to cope because I realized they were doing more harm, but I had no healthy alternatives. My depression just became more and more severe.

As I've said, at Professor Palmer's insistence, I searched for a therapist online. It was such a relief that he took the time to listen to my story and get to know me, instead of simply dumping me at the counseling center as two professors previously had.

When searching for a therapist, I didn't have high hopes, but I found Kelly, and Kelly saved my life. I know this sounds very dramatic and I do my best not to be, but nothing short of that statement could encompass what working with her has done for me. (After reading this, Kelly has told me that she did not save my life and that I saved my own life. Maybe I saved my own life, but Kelly had a starring role.) Therapy has given me a chance to express my feelings with no judgement or shame.

The first time we met was the last Tuesday before I started student teaching. I took the bus to her office and thought about getting off and taking the next bus home. I had told my professor about my appointment, and it was the thought of having to tell him that I hadn't gone which pushed me to enter the waiting room. I waited in a tiny room with a few chairs and magazines. I filled out some paperwork that was waiting for me in an envelope and read about Bindi Irwin in *People*. I was about 15 minutes early, as I am to most things, and the waiting was torture. Finally, Kelly came out and she looked as kind as her picture. She asked me if I wanted water and I knew I would need it. My mouth gets very dry when I talk about difficult things or have anxiety. Does this happen to anyone else?

We went to her office and it felt like a safe space. The large window helped me not to feel trapped and I sat on a cream couch across from her. She sat on an armchair. We made a tiny bit of small talk and this made me more comfortable, but five minutes in I was already halfway through my water. She asked me about how I had decided to come in and I told her about my story.

"Well, I wrote this story for a creative writing class and my professor realized it was about something that actually happened to me and he helped me a lot, but he also thought I should see a therapist, so here I am."

We talked for a few minutes about the story and my professor, but I couldn't bring myself to say what the story was actually about. Kelly finally said, "Are we going to beat around this? Or are you going to say what happened in the story?" Writing that it doesn't sound very nice, but she said it in her kind way. I probably replied, "I was sexually assaulted," because saying the words "I was raped," was beyond me at this time and, as I have said, sometimes still is.

The gate had opened and I began talking. I told her everything. The rape. The case. Court. The case against me. Everything. Like with Professor Palmer, we didn't go into details about anything too deeply, I just gave her the timeline and I told her those horrible phrases from the Vice President of Student Affairs.

We started meeting once a week and it helped my anxiety, depression, and vaginismus. I learned coping skills like breathing techniques and using essential oils and things with strong scents when I start to panic. I also learned how to talk through what had happened to me and feel no shame or responsibility.

At first, it was embarrassing to talk about being suicidal and I didn't want to bring it up. I felt like I was admitting some sort of failure. But the more I talked to Kelly about it, the less embarrassed I felt. As I started to face this challenge and others, suicide began to feel like less and less of an option. During our first few months of working together, we had scheduled email check-ins in between sessions. I was actively suicidal and this helped keep me safe.

I was also embarrassed to bring up the cutting. I wasn't cutting as much as I had in the past, but it was hard to stop altogether. It helped a lot that once I brought it up to her, she explained how common cutting was for people who had been through things like I'd been through, and it was only after we worked on the causes for my cutting that I was finally able to truly stop.

Sometimes when things get hard, it can be difficult to stop myself from cutting again, but I am honest with Kelly about when I feel the urge and I have not cut myself since graduating.

My body had associated the feeling of lying down in a bed with being raped, and this was not easy to change. We worked through a bedtime routine and I started to make sure to spend time in bed reading before going to sleep. This has helped me to associate my bed as a safe space and not a place to dread, and I no long feel debilitating fear of the darkness.

When I graduated, we decided it would be helpful to continue our sessions when I moved back to Boston, so now we FaceTime. There's nothing off limits to talk about and I feel stronger than I thought I could be. Therapy has also helped me in my everyday life as a teacher and girlfriend. Kelly helped me when my grandma died and every time I've been rejected from a job. I have laughed and cried during therapy, sometimes in the same session. I have learned how to exercise safely and not starve myself. I still struggle to not be too hard on myself about grades and I cried both times I got a B on a paper in graduate school. I am a work in progress.

Yes, things started to get easier once I started therapy, but it was still a hard road. I had never been able to process what had happened to me and it was overwhelming to face it all. I was finally able to grieve for myself and this was painful, but necessary. I had to grieve for everything I had lost. I guess I had to grieve for the version of myself that no longer existed and my view of the world that had been shattered. Grieving helped lead me to acceptance and in that I was truly able to start healing.

It took about a year for me to say his name in a session, and saying the actual words, "Noah Silverman raped me" was incredibly empowering. It was like saying, "This really happened, and it matters." Well, I didn't actually say those words because his name is something different, but you get what I mean.

Words like "victim" and "survivor" can make me uncomfortable. I'm just a person. Therapy helped me reinvent my identity, as it had been tied to what happened to me for too long. In sessions, we often refer to me at that time as "victim Laurie" and we honor all that she did.

The fall after graduation, Kelly and I decided that medication would be helpful. I made an appointment with my primary care doctor and told her about my anxiety and depression. I got a prescription for Zoloft or, actually, the cheaper generic version. I had been stuck in high anxiety and depression for years, and my brain needed help to get out of this. I don't think medication is the be-all and end-all, but with therapy it helped my anxiety no longer be debilitating and my depression wasn't as heavy. I do not understand why we don't bat an eye when people take Robitussin for a cough or get a cast for a broken arm, but there has to be a debate about getting medical help for your mental health. If you think you need medication, it is your life and you have to do what you can to thrive.

Soon after returning to Boston, I even met with a nutritionist and truly learned how to take care of and nourish myself.

When I visited Chicago in the summer of 2016, Kelly and I had an in-person session. It was so nice to see a full-sized Kelly and not just an image on my iPad. We talked for a while and then we watched the documentary film, *The Hunting Ground*. This film opened my eyes to the system that I had been a victim of. It wasn't just me. Women and men across the country are told not to go to the police when they are sexually assaulted and are then silenced by their universities.

If you have not seen this film, I highly recommend that you watch it. I cannot stress enough how important it is to understand that what happened to me happens all the time.

The part of the film that made me cry was learning about Lizzy Seeberg's suicide. She committed suicide 10 days after she was raped. Or I guess I have to say "allegedly" raped, which is infuriating. She was a college freshman when she was (allegedly) raped, just like me. Lizzy reported her (alleged) rape to campus police, but her (alleged) rapist wasn't interviewed until she had been dead for five days. Every story is different, of course, but our society has allowed men and women to get away with unimaginable actions because we refuse to believe victims and colleges believe helping their students will tarnish their reputations.

I am grateful that I was able to watch this film in a safe place with Kelly and she has helped me when I've been triggered by similar stories, like Bill Cosby (who did get three to 10 years in jail, but let's not pat ourselves on the back; he was facing up to 30 years in prison). Like Brock Turner (who could have been sentenced to six years in prison, but served just three months). Like the myriad of sexual crimes in Hollywood and the workplace. Like Larry Nassar and his disgusting reign of sexual assaults (332. He assaulted at least 332 girls and women! You don't assault that many people without A LOT of help covering it up). Like Kavanaugh and the way the hearing tore the US apart, and seeing how survivors were forced to question when and if it is okay to share what they have been through. Even our President, Trump, who has been accused of sexual misconduct by multiple women and has publicly mocked survivors and shamed us for not reporting. I talk to Kelly about how the actions of these people have made me feel and I do not have to carry my story and the stories of others alone.

My best advice, if you are thinking of seeing a therapist, is do your research. And if one therapist doesn't work out, find a new one. Therapists are people and you don't click with every person you meet, so you won't click with every therapist. Most importantly, stick with it. It isn't always fun, but it's your life and you are worth it.

# CHAPTER 22

# The Loss

Today, I know that rape and sex are not the same thing. Rape is an act of violence. It's not about sex. It really is about having power over another person. For me though, it's not so "simple". If it was not obvious (and it's mentioned more than once, so come on) I'd never had sex when I was raped. I guess you could say I was a virgin, and for some reason I don't like to use that word because it has a lot of connotations and it makes you think about sex. It's one of those words that feels so awkward to say and never gets brought up in conversation, but for lack of a better word, I was a virgin.

Today, I know that what was done to me was not sex. It was violence that happened to use certain body parts, but coming to this realization was not easy.

The idea of virginity can be so powerful and meaningful. At least it was to me. I had an idea of what I wanted: someone who I loved and who made me feel safe. I hadn't met that person yet, but I felt they were out there and that my first time would be meaningful. Maybe that sounds naive. Friends I've spoken to about this have assured me that their first times were awkward and sometimes painful and not a "fairytale". But they had the dignity and choice to be with that person, whether it was perfect or not.

The pain of losing the opportunity to have a first time with someone I cared for and chose to be with was devastating. The day after I was raped, when I was talking to Sarah about what happened, I had this moment of realization: *I'm not a virgin anymore.* It hadn't hit me so strongly yet. I was incredibly nauseous (from a mixture of my hangover, Plan B, and just the whole thing) and I was afraid that if I threw up I would need to get another dose. Sitting on my bed and feeling the overwhelming shame and sadness from myself and judgement from Sarah, I began to feel like crying. I didn't let myself cry just yet, because I was so embarrassed to cry in front of Sarah and for her to make another comment about how I had simply done something I now regretted. I told her I needed to go the bathroom and when the door was safely locked, I cried while clutching my nails into my palms and willing the nausea to pass. That caring and safe vision of my first time was gone. Ripped away.

That day and for the next couple of weeks, the physical pain was constant and excruciating. I bled for days – either from the rape or from the emergency hormones – and the sight of it made me cry all over again. The pain was a horrible reminder of the loss, and once it lessened it didn't truly leave for years. In those first few weeks, I cried for hours over my confusion and sadness and what that horrible pain meant. As I have said, the cutting didn't take long to be a constant in my life. Some days I would sit on my bed staring at the opposite wall, feeling utterly numb. Other days I would lay in bed with the covers over my head, just crying and hoping my roommates couldn't hear me. When that felt unbearable, I would go to the bathroom, lock myself in a stall, and cut myself with shaking hands.

The self-blame over the whole thing only made the loss of my virginity that much more devastating. The emotions and turmoil surrounding all that happened tore me apart inside. I didn't want to be myself anymore and I wanted out. I was not seriously suicidal at this point yet, but during this time was when the seed was planted. I had never felt this way before and just the thought of it scared me. I was afraid of what I was capable of.

I started to use the Rape, Abuse & Incest National Network (RAINN) online chat daily, and it made those first few months bearable. Through this chat I was able to talk with a trained volunteer in a non-judgemental space. And I wasn't forced to label what I had gone through. No, I was not able to face that I had been raped yet, but just having someone to talk it out with and to listen was so helpful. I didn't bring up that I had been a virgin and I didn't call what happened rape, I just shared the facts as I could remember them. I don't think I mentioned being suicidal, but when thoughts later became much stronger, I used the National Suicide Prevention Lifeline online chat. This chat was similar to the RAINN chat and it truly helped me to share my feelings and not be completely alone. These two online chats were so invaluable during this time in my life. The first time I used them I felt a little embarrassed and apprehensive, but the people I spoke to (or wrote to) were such kind listeners and they gave practical advice.

When I finally got help, even in therapy, I felt embarrassed to disclose that I had never had sex when I was raped. There can be shame either way – you've had sex so you're a slut or you haven't had sex, so what the hell is wrong with you? There was nothing wrong with me. I hadn't found the right person and I wasn't ready. It was hard to face up to what this extra layer of trauma meant. Once I finally brought this up in therapy, I grieved for the loss and the version of my first time that could never happen.

In a way, being in denial that Noah had raped me let me hold onto a version of reality where I hadn't had my virginity stolen; I had had consensual sex, and like Sarah said, "I now regretted it". Whether I could recognize that I had been raped or not, I was certain that it was my fault. The idea of this version of that night (that I had had sex I now regretted) was toxic and my denial only led to more self-hatred. It was this idea that made it so difficult for me to go forward with the case through the school, and that made me write off the harassment until it went to a terrifying level. Even after Noah threatened me on the street, I still felt confused over it all and blamed myself. I convinced myself that he didn't think he had raped me, and he was harassing me to keep me quiet and to keep himself from getting in trouble. Beyond that, I wasn't so sure I had been raped either. So then it really was all my fault.

While talking to different friends, I have found out that two of them had been raped (which was shocking in itself, and made me sad again that we all kept this from each other). And they were raped when they were virgins. I don't wish this on anyone, but being able to talk about this with them has helped me not feel so alone. I wish that I could tell my 18-year-old self that what happened was not her fault and that she would heal and be able to have all the experiences she wanted. I know that therapy and acceptance helped me get here, and the way I felt in the past is so foreign to me, it's hard to imagine feeling that lost and hopeless.

I will never have experiences that aren't in some way clouded by this, and that can feel really defeating and isolating. I am very grateful, though, that therapy has helped me tremendously with this. Therapy also helped me separate consensual sex from rape, and I learned to identify what felt safe.

I had to decide that though I was raped as a virgin, I could still take ownership over my first consensual experience and all experiences going forward. The mental and physical scars are still here, but they don't define me.

# CHAPTER 23

## Coming to Chicago

I almost didn't make it to Chicago my freshman year. Hurricane Irene was blazing through the East Coast, but that was only part of the problem. I blame Lara Bars. The cheapest flights are usually early in the morning and our flight to Chicago, on August 26, 2011, was at 6:00am. Not boarding at 6:00am, departing at 6:00am. Well maybe not 6:00am on the dot, but pretty close. I am a lot of things, but a morning person is not one of them. My dad has ingrained in my family that for a flight leaving at 3:00 in the afternoon, you'd best get to the airport at 12:30pm. That day, we were not that family sitting at the gate for two hours. I had to make sure all my things were in order and, with little sleep, my family was not moving too quickly. I must have looked terrible because my sister asked me, "Are you wearing purple eyeliner?"

I found out that I was accepted to my school by receiving a giant yellow envelope in the mail that said the words, "You've Been Admitted," in huge print on the outside of the envelope. I didn't even have to open it to know the good news. I got my letter late one afternoon in March of my senior year of high school. I was watching a special on TV about ghosts in Key West with my mom, when my dad came in with the mail. Key West is ridiculously haunted, if you believe in that sort of thing.

When I saw the letter in my dad's hand I was ecstatic, and I started jumping up and down with my parents. I called my sister and Sarah and they were excited too. Since I had decided to apply at the last minute, I had never visited my school or even Chicago. A few weeks after my acceptance, my dad and I visited the city and the school and I fell in love. I confirmed my acceptance and imagined myself strolling down Michigan Avenue with my new college friends.

Over the next few months, I geared myself up for going to college and being away from home. My mom and I went to Marshalls and bought a comforter, extra-long sheets, and other dorm essentials. I graduated from high school a few days after my 18th birthday and was ready for the next phase of my life.

For whatever reason, Logan airport was crowded the morning we were leaving that August, and security was taking forever. My family each had a suitcase filled with my stuff and my dad's carry-on was devoted to my snacks. My mom had bought me an abundance of nuts, protein powder, and a whole case of Lara Bars. When my dad's carry-on went through the scanner, it was pulled to the side and inspected. The TSA guards asked him about the contents of his bag and the bars, and as my mom had packed it, my dad answered the questions as best he could.

During this important interrogation, our flight boarded and left. No more flights would be leaving for Chicago that day because of Irene, but there was a flight to New York City and the potential to fly from New York to Chicago. We took a chance and flew to New York. When we landed, we waited to see if the scheduled flight to Chicago would be able to take off, and after a few hours we got the go-ahead.

In Chicago, we stayed in a hotel in the Gold Coast neighborhood and I tried not to think about my family leaving in a couple days. My family helped me set up my things in the dorm and I dreaded the moment they would really leave. We didn't have time to go around the city, but we did see a play and it was incredibly depressing. On my family's last day in town, my dad and sister explored a bit and my mom and I worked tirelessly to make sure my room was in order. I was the first of my roommates to arrive and I was anxious to meet them. My mom and I worked through lunch and by dinner time we were hungry and exhausted. My sister and dad came back and we went to the McDonald's around the corner from my dorm. Outside of McDonald's, my sister saw a man get his briefcase stolen.

"Don't tell Mom," I told her.

My mom is very good at worrying and she was already convinced that Chicago was not a safe place. Any city or town has good and bad people and I have seen people get robbed in Boston.

I did not tell my mom when a man came to my apartment building two nights in a row with a chainsaw to steal bikes from the bike rack out front (yes, I called the police, no, they didn't do anything) and I begrudgingly told her when my iPhone was stolen out of my purse at that bar. I called the police then too and they were certain that I had just lost it. In my experience purses usually don't unzip themselves and iPhones don't jump out. I told my parents about the attempted break-in, mainly because I was worried about Sarah and yes, I called the police and they did nothing.

I struggle with the fact that my parents only know about my rape ... or actually I don't even know what they know, because as you may recall, the Dean called my parents to tell them about it, probably in a ploy to get me to drop out. But I don't actually know what he said to them. And to him I was only an *alleged* rape victim and eventually a liar, so I really have no idea what he told them.

My parents and I have never discussed it, and this is what I am comfortable with. Maybe if I had been able to tell them when I was ready, things would be different, but that was taken from me. I will say that once I decided to share with my parents about writing this book (I didn't tell them about this book until it was going to be published), they were incredibly supportive. Maybe this is a chance to have the conversations that we never had and for me to be able to share my experience with them.

I did eventually go to the police when the harassment started, and I even reported my rape, but again nothing.

When it was time to leave Chicago after my graduation it was storming terribly, and with flash floods my flight was delayed. My parents had come to see me graduate and pack my things, and we sat in the airport as our takeoff time kept getting later and later. My dad and I walked through the airport to try to combat our boredom. I was starting to doubt that our flight would take off and this doubt was fueled when we saw workers setting up row after row of cots. It looked like a quarantine. It was seeming like our flight would be canceled

and I thought about how it strange it was that I almost had not made it to Chicago and now Chicago would not let me leave.

My last term at school was amazing. I got to student teach half in a preschool class and half in a second-grade class. On Monday nights I had my student teaching seminar and it felt so good to see the ladies I had taken my classes with for four years and to discuss how teaching was going. The weather got warmer and I went on walks along Lake Michigan and went shopping with Polly. I started going to therapy once a week and it became an important part of my healing.

*A bittersweet night at 360 Chicago, before I said goodbye to the city.*

127

I did touristy things that you don't do when you live somewhere, especially when you don't feel safe, like going to see The Bean (I just googled this and apparently its official name is Cloud Gate), visiting The Art Institute and the John Hancock Observatory. I had an amazing birthday / end of student teaching party and it was nice to see all of the friends that I made in Chicago. I saw the musical *Once* at the Cadillac Palace Theatre and my family went out for hibachi on the night of my graduation. I was sad to leave. I wished it had been like that for more of my time in this incredible city. Our flight did eventually leave and I was relieved, but a little sad that I wouldn't have one more night in Chicago. In a hotel, obviously – no way was I going to sleep on one of those cots.

# CHAPTER 24

# Forgiveness?

I don't know what to say about forgiveness. In a psychology class in graduate school, I came face to face with forgiveness and it was not pretty. The lecture talked about how people who cannot forgive are weak, that you need to abandon your right to resentment, and your place in the "victim role". The lecture had other points too that were less harsh, but these were the statements that stuck with me. I really liked this class and the professor, and I was a bit shocked by this lecture. I felt like I was being attacked, but there's no way she could have known it would trigger me. The class always had us discuss prompts during the lecture and on this day, I was partnered with two guys in the class. Not partnered, but whatever the word is when you have two partners. The two guys went about discussing forgiveness and the lecture material, and I felt like if I opened my mouth to say a word I would cry. Our professor came over and asked, "Laurie, what do you think?"

"I'm feeling really emotional, so I can't talk about it right now." Damn. Here come the tears. My professor looked uncomfortable and had the class wrap up their discussions.

One of my partners was really nice about it and asked if I was okay, telling me that I didn't need to share anything if

I didn't want to. This made me feel less bad about being the crazy person who cried in class.

I have learned to stick up for myself over the years and I am especially good at this when it's through email. I emailed my professor about the content that troubled me. I am in a pretty good place now, but if I had heard that lecture a few years ago it would have hurt me much more. I also thought that it wasn't implausible that someone else in the class had similar feelings and it's more likely than not that at least one student in every university class will have been raped. Statistically it's probably more than that.

My professor had a nice enough response to my email, which was kind of along the lines of, "I am sorry that the lecture bothered you, but not about the content." She said I could meet with her to discuss which slides were of concern to me, but I did not feel I could do this without outing myself. I am still proud that I sent her that email, regardless of the outcome.

Without further ado, here are my feelings on forgiveness:

Do I believe that we should not hold grudges? Yes. Do I believe that some people benefit from forgiving those that have wronged them? Probably. Will I ever forgive my rapist? No, but I don't actively hate him either. I'd feel better if he was in jail or had been expelled; I'd even feel a bit better if the suspension had stuck. But I guess that would be too much to ask for. I know this is really unhealthy and I have not done this in at least a year, but I used to periodically look up Noah on Facebook. How else would I know he transferred? His profile is full of stories of him cooking for friends, photos of him smiling, and musings about life. Yes, the lives people portray on social media are carefully constructed, but sometimes his apparent happiness stings a little. At this point though, I rarely think of Noah and I doubt he thinks of me.

I don't hate Sarah either. I feel a kind of indifference towards her that I feel towards most of my friends and acquaintances that I didn't keep in contact with after high school or college.

I used to feel responsible for what happened to her and would wish that I had stayed at the party even though she was screaming at me. What happened to Sarah was not my fault and what happened to me was not her fault either.

Do I hate my school? The short answer is no. In some ways I loved my time in college. I learned a lot, had incredible professors, made friends, and got to intern at schools all over the city.

I don't hate the Dean of Students either. He probably did what he thought was right for the school and that's who he wanted to protect. I also think in his own way he tried to help me, but that was not his priority.

I still remember sitting in the Dean's office at one of our meetings and feeling tired and defeated. I was staring at my jeans, noticing how they had become faded and wondering when that had happened. I couldn't bear to look him in the eye.

"What class do you have next?" He had asked me.

"Archaeology. It's for a history credit."

"That sounds fun. How are you liking the class?"

I looked up and met his kind smile, and suddenly I didn't feel so embarrassed. I felt like a person. He could be caring and I don't think this was completely an act. Yet, I feel for all of the women and men that have had to be tricked and humiliated by this man, by their universities, and by society. It's hard to imagine him receiving my email begging to know what was going on with the case against me and that he had it in him to ignore me. It is also devastating to think that he was a part of the case, but I think him being a part of it is only logical. The first red flag about his true colors should have been how interested he was in how much I had had to drink that night and if my friends had been smoking cigarettes or weed when they went to the park. I asked him if that mattered and he assured me it did. Guess what? It didn't.

I looked up the Dean recently and discovered that he is now the Dean of Students at another large university. I also discovered that since my rape he has written publications on sexual violence and mental health deterioration in university students. He's taken multiple trainings on sexual violence and rape. He's even written about how colleges need to change their approach to rape and hearings. Interesting. It's hard for me to believe that he could change that much, and I wonder if this is for show or if maybe someone has a guilty conscience. I also do wonder if this is a sign of changing times. If you are in position of power, you always have an opportunity to be a helper and not a hurter and you can always change the way you conduct yourself. Maybe he really did realize that protecting a school at all costs was not how he wanted to live his life. If he has changed, maybe this shows that deans and schools can change. Things don't have to continue the way they are.

The only person that I still feel much of anything towards is the Vice President of Student Affairs. What she did was calculated and benefited no one, but I guess it's in the past. I really cannot say I hate her either. Not hating someone, though, does not equal forgiveness.

In my creative writing class, we read a story about a man who killed someone by accident in his youth. I was feeling triggered by my own life when I read this story, so I couldn't be impartial during our class discussion. People do make horrible mistakes. The man in this story suffered for years for what he did in a sort of futuristic prison that tested drugs on the inmates. I couldn't feel compassion towards him when I read it, but I know now that making a mistake does not make you a bad person, and one bad action does not make you a bad person either. Intent is important. I don't understand how people can hurt each other in such violent and atrocious ways.

Ryan was murdered in Chicago in 2015 at the age of 24. He was shot in the chest and left for dead. He had looked out for Sarah and me at parties and would always text to make sure we made it home okay. He was a person with his life in front of him and then he was gone. If someone makes a choice to rape or kill or something like that, I believe that is different.

Forgiveness is not black and white. You are not weak if you cannot forgive, but remember that holding on to your pain will only hurt you, not the person who did the hurting. In a way, I had to forgive myself by realizing there was nothing to forgive, and I had to allow myself the space and safety to express my emotions and not get mad at myself for how I felt. Forgiveness is about letting go of the idea that the past can be changed. I didn't come up with that; I think that was one of the better points from the lecture. If you want to forgive, forgive, but do it because you want to, not because you feel you have to. Honor the good and the bad times. The past cannot be changed, but you can change your future.

# CHAPTER 25

## Journal

For my creative writing class, we had to keep a journal and write in it every day. Every. Single. Day. So, at the start of the term, I went to my school's bookstore and bought an overpriced blue notebook and put a pink post-it on the cover that read, "Do Not Forget Me on Thursdays!"

Writing in our journals was supposed to help us get used to writing, and in our journals we could write about whatever we wanted. Professor Palmer would then check our pages to see that we were writing, but not read them. My journal is like an account of that time and all of my conflicting feelings.

Here some snippets from the journal that I kept for my creative writing class.

### January 8, 2015

Kind of having a nervous breakdown right now. Remembering launching rockets in ninth grade. Not actually launching them, I have no memory of that. Waiting to launch them. Not who was there, but what it felt like, just waiting. Was I sitting? Was I standing? I can't remember. Creative writing might have been the wrong choice. I can do this. I can do this. I can do this. I can do this. There will come a day when I will look back on everything and barely remember the whole thing. Just a few memories will stick out. Like that time waiting to launch rockets in ninth grade physics. Random images and feelings stick out and you don't know why. I love myself and I can't undo the past. I am a good person. I can do this. I will sleep well tonight.

**January 10, 2015**

Why does writing make me so sad? I get in this weird depressed mood and I just want to fill these pages. I'm thinking of that time that I took that express train to Howard by accident and missed my internship and that guy told this girl's father that the man's daughter dropped out of high school and it was just a couple months before graduation. The father had no idea his daughter dropped out. I wonder what happened to that girl and why she dropped out. I was so excited for this class. I've planned to take it for years, so why is it such a struggle now? It is important to challenge yourself. I will grow from this experience and I am not the same person I was all those years ago and that's a good thing.

**January 12, 2015**

I love looking out the window and seeing this cute little Yorkie walking around with his cute little white dog friend. Such happy puppies!

**January 13, 2015**

I'm still struggling with my writing assignments. I am afraid that I'm going to fail. It seems so easy for my classmates. I watched *Dead Poets Society* last night and it really got to me. I think for growth you need to challenge yourself. I'm so original. Writing is harder than I thought it would be.

**January 17, 2015**

Maybe I'm so reserved in this class because I have so much inside of me that if I let it out, if I remove the lid, I may never be able to get it back on. I have so much inside of me. I'm feeling better today. The weather has been less horrific, and it feels almost like spring. Literally so over writing in this. It's actually the 20th and I'm actively resenting having to write in this damn journal.

**January 20, 2015**

I really love my internship and it just feels right to be there. I hope things stay good and I just want to feel happy and I feel happy today. I got my new boots! So cute and comfy and I can't wait to wear them to class.

**January 22, 2015**

Class is okay, I guess. It's interesting and I think I'm writing okay stuff. I'm just tired of this. And I think one day I might just end it and that feels kind of okay. I think about this a lot and I know how I would do it and some days it's like I never left the laundry room and I'm still telling myself I can either kill myself or go to class and when will the day come that going to class doesn't win?

**January 27, 2015**

It's kind of weird that a page is blank and then it can never go back to what it was. Once you add something it's changed forever. I always leave for my internship at the same time, so I always see the same people on the bus. But yesterday, it was basically empty and I saw no regulars. Like the person that really stands out is this woman who always looks like she's wearing expensive boots and she has a nice bag and a Starbucks. On Friday she had a suitcase. She always gets off at Ravenswood which is kind of funny and makes me think of the failed *Pretty Little Liars* spin-off. So, on Friday, no different, she got off at Ravenswood with her suitcase and I thought, she's leaving straight from work for vacation or something. She sat next to me on the bus once for a few stops and then when more seats opened she moved, which kind of offended me and was kind of a relief, because who likes sitting next to anyone on the bus? So, Starbucks lady had an excuse to not be there on Monday, but where was everyone else? Kind of hating noticing things so much lately. Ever since I've been writing a lot. Deep people can be super annoying.

**January 30, 2015**

One day a snowflake fell. It was the only one. It jumped early forgetting its brothers and sisters. It just wanted to feel the earth. It jumped from a cloud and melted before it hit the ground. Yeah, why does this poem sound pretentious and terrible?

**February 1, 2015**

I appreciate: the sun, the moon, blue skies, the ability to go to college, my parents, my sister, hot water, cold water, Pure Barre, Pure Barre socks, playing tennis with my dad, sunglasses, cars, planes, Chicago, Boston, smiling, eating, running, face wash, contacts, glasses, leggings, Advil, sitting, standing, walking, looking to the future, the ability to read and write, my mom and dad again because I love them so much and I feel like crying because I can never show or express how much I love them, books, cameras, my phone, the ability to learn and change, capital and lowercase letters, Chapstick, water, teaching, getting to student teach, learning from and accepting struggles, *Taken 3* because it's hilarious at this point.

**February 2, 2015**

I need to go to bed. It's so late. But I don't want to be in the dark. I've been okay with this for a while, but tonight the dark doesn't feel right and I don't want to have nightmares and I'm tired, but going to bed means being in the dark and the dark is when I don't feel safe and sometimes that doesn't make sense to me because it wasn't all dark when it happened. He had his bedside light on. But it's like those feelings and my fear are waiting in the dark and then I'm in his bed and he's on top of me and I can't move. I don't know if I can do it tonight.

**February 3, 2015**

I do not need to keep following this destructive pattern. The next phase of my life is coming, I'm going to graduate. I really wish it was warmer. I always end up back on this couch and it's like do I ever leave? Do not let the bad stuff consume you. It was so long ago. It shouldn't matter.

### February 4, 2015

I wrote a story for my creative writing final story and it's basically finished, but I just can't connect to it and like it is really different and kind of sci-fi, I guess and then the main girl gets raped and like ...

So, I started writing about the hearing, but as this character version of me and of everything else as a flashback, but then the flashback just became the story. I've basically finished writing it. I know I'll keep adding to it and editing and changing it because I can't leave things alone. But I wrote it. And I created Lindy and I made her go into his bedroom and be grateful. And I made her drunk and flattered. And I made her tell him he could take her bra off. And I made her cry. And I made it painful. And I made her think she was going to die. And then, I made her die. Am I doing this? Am I turning this story in? I have the other one good to go. But this is my story, and no one will ever know about it and no one will ever care about it. And I wish someone cared about it, even if they only care about Lindy.

### February 5, 2015

How good is honey? And chocolate? And tea? And hot packs? Just a few more lines to fill this page.

### February 6, 2015

Being silenced is killing me.

### February 8, 2015

Sometimes I wonder if Noah ever thinks of me. As I write this, he's doing something. He went to bed last night and had something for dinner. He watches TV and worries about the future. He discovers new songs on the radio and randomly thinks of things he did in high school.

**February 9, 2015**

Do people really change? At first, they seem different, but when you look more closely … I saw Stan, Sarah's … boyfriend? From the beginning of sophomore year. At the beginning of the term, I hung out with him and Aurora and before this I had no idea they were still in contact. I hadn't seen him since his roommate's boyfriend went crazy right before Thanksgiving sophomore year and punched out him and that girl that he was cheating on Sarah with. So, Aurora wanted to hang out and said that Stan would pick me up at my apartment and I assumed that Stan was some guy she was seeing and when I got in the car I didn't recognize him because he had shaved his head. Then he said, "Hello Laurie, it's been a while." And I was like, *holy shit, it's Stan.* He seemed so different for most of the ride. He talked about how he used to only want to buy things and make money. But, as the ride went on, he showed himself to be just as materialistic and narcissistic as ever. He was complaining about working at that club and wanting to quit – which was the case two years ago – and trashing the people that go there. He had seemed so evolved at first, but now he just hides his shittiness better.

When he knew me, we would go to his apartment and get wasted on a Wednesday night. He snuck me into clubs and taught me how to smoke cigarettes. In the car ride to Aurora's I asked him if I seemed different and he said I seemed the same. I'm not the same. This whole time I've questioned everything that has been defining my life and who I am. I really have changed. I'm still confused, but I've changed. Or have I just gotten better at hiding things about myself? I don't think that's it. Stan was a terrifying driver. We had usually been drinking when he drove us and really at the time that was thrilling. Being in his car this time I felt afraid. And I think being afraid of actually dying may be a good sign.

At my core I'm the same person, but I'm stronger. I don't get drunk most nights of the week. I hardly drink at all. I'm better to myself and I'm not okay, but I think I'll be okay and back then I didn't think okay was an option.

**February 10, 2015**

Really miss Sarah suddenly. The thought that this is permanent. That she's really gone. I just never thought it would go on forever. Everything has me super worked up today. Probably because, well, people can really suck sometimes.

**February 11, 2015**

I'm just so excited for the good part to start. I'm happy now, happier I guess but this can't be it. Roku, why are you just the best thing ever? Did I mention the guy down the hall gave us his old TV? Amazing.

**February 12, 2015**

What if I actually died that May 29th? May 29th this year is my last day of student teaching and that night I'm planning an end of student teaching / birthday party.

**February 13, 2015**

Lindy is dead and I need to let her go. She's dead. Let her go. I couldn't protect her and now she's dead. Why couldn't I protect myself? Why wouldn't he stop? Why didn't I say s top? Why was I grateful when he let me lie down? Grateful. Why did I drink so much? Why did Sarah leave me? Why didn't I go to the police? Why did I go to the Dean? Why couldn't I push him off of me? Why did it have to hurt so much? It hurt so much. Why does it still hurt? Why didn't they believe me? Why did he hold me down? Why am I still alive? She's dead. Let her go.

**February 15, 2015**

It's not what I imagined for my first time. When everyone came back and he went to greet them and I was alone and getting dressed, I kind of remember looking around his room for something to clean myself off with, but I can't remember if I did that or not. I remember putting on my jeans and that burning and I don't think I was crying and that feels strange. I guess I had a task to complete and I think I went to the bathroom before leaving the apartment and I'm pretty sure I threw up. No, I'm sure I did because I got it in my hair and this made me cry.

**February 17, 2015**

My story is due today. The first draft. It's hard because it's *my* story. I just don't know the reaction I'll get. You just never know how people will react. You can't control another person. You could never look through the lens that they do. Or know how their experiences have shaped their point of view. I have spent so much time working on it and changing it and adding details. I have to stop editing and adding, but I can always find something to fix. It needed to be true or it wouldn't matter. What if they say she consented? Or think she wanted it? What if they think it was her fault? Then it was my fault.

**February 19, 2015**

Thursday. My story is supposed to be discussed today and I'm not sure how I feel about that.

**February 20, 2015**

My story wasn't discussed … I'm having a lot of feelings. Really want to go to Wicker Park, but it's cold and gross out. I've loved writing and I feel like when this class is over I'll never write again and that makes me sad. I've learned so much. I don't know what I want for my story. If it will give me any peace. I just don't know anymore. I can't let it go. I don't know how to. I'm so confused about the truth. I don't know. I have to let this go. I just need to be heard. My story didn't get discussed and it's making me more nervous.

**February 23, 2015**

I need this to matter and it doesn't matter. Only to me and that doesn't mean much.

## February 25, 2015

Will my story be discussed tomorrow? People might hate it. They might tear it apart. They might blame Lindy. I think of the memories that I have. The flashes and feelings. The smells and music. His face, that look on his face. Sometimes I wish I could remember it all and sometimes I wish I could forget the whole thing.

## February 26, 2015

My story was discussed. I don't know how to process this. My professor figured out it was real. He talked to me after class and he believed me. He actually believed me. And it was okay. Kind of embarrassing when I think about it too much, but it was okay. I feel like I can breathe. He listened to it all and he believed me. And I really think he believes me.

## February 27, 2015

Just want to be a normal 21-year-old.

## March 2, 2015

Everything is changing. My view of everything has changed. Maybe writing out what I wrote out helped me and I'm having these realizations. Yes, I made mistakes, but I'm not responsible for what happened. I think it was when we were discussing my story in class and no one blamed Lindy. It was like they were telling me it wasn't my fault. I even included the things I said, and no one took them to see Lindy as a slut or responsible. They saw her in the playground. Saw *me* in the playground and that she wasn't trying to do anything bad. She was inexperienced, naive, and her friends let her down. I need to accept the truth and my story is the truth. I know I'm going to be okay. I can't explain the relief. It all comes down to the bra. That was in the story too and it was okay. I feel like a weight has been lifted. I didn't even realize this thing was weighing me down so badly. I feel okay. I'm going to be okay. I know I'm going to be okay.

**March 3, 2015**

I slept pretty well last night and I didn't have any nightmares. It's so refreshing to feel well rested.

**March 4, 2015**

I need to forgive myself. No. I need to realize that I have nothing to forgive myself for. It wasn't my fault.

**March 5, 2015**

It wasn't my fault.

**March 6, 2015**

Letting go is never easy. I can't imagine what I'd be like, what my life would've been like if things had been different four years ago. Like it still happened, but he was held accountable and everyone believed me. Or he wasn't even held accountable, but no one thought I was a liar. Why does him not being held accountable mean that I automatically am a liar? I'm actually getting pretty sad about this being my last week of writing in this journal. I feel like crying, but over what?

**March 7, 2015**

The finality of these pages is freaking me out. When the final pages are done, they're done. Closing one chapter to open another. This is a good thing. Going out with Polly tonight because why not?

**March 8, 2015**

I wrote an amazing story. I did that.

**March 9, 2015**

When I read this journal in a year or five years or ten years, will I be able to believe the darkness of this time? What does your life look like now, future Laurie? The sun is shining and it's 5:30 in the afternoon. Spring always comes after winter.

**March 10, 2015**

I had my first appointment with my therapist. I think it went really, really well. She's so nice and easy to talk to. I think this will be a good thing. I really have a good feeling about this. Like I didn't feel awkward. There were no awkward pauses. She just kept the conversation flowing. And her office is huge with a huge window. So, it's all good. I just got a spray deodorant to try something new, so let's see where this goes, shall we?

**March 11, 2015**

Spray deodorants are terrible.

**March 12, 2015**

Final Thursday. Love yourself. It's all waiting for you.

# CHAPTER 26

# Graduation

A Hail Mary Pass is a really long forward pass in football, or I should say American football. It is a desperate attempt that rarely works and it is usually employed when time is about to run out. As my Hail Mary Pass, I had a final plan to change my legacy at my school: be the graduation speaker. Or at least the graduation speaker for the College of Education, as each college had a separate graduation. I got an email saying that there was a speech contest and the person with the best speech would get to be the speaker.

At my high school, the graduation speaker was chosen pretty much the same way. I wrote my speech in my public speaking class and my teacher who was caring and helpful encouraged me to audition. There were actually two speakers chosen and I was one of them. It was amazing to be one of the graduation speakers. I worked hard on my speech and got to audition in front of English teachers and the deans at my high school. I had a pretty good high school experience, as far as high school experiences go. I had my group of friends, the chance to take interesting classes, and amazing teachers. My principal was a really cool guy who preached freedom and responsibility and almost six years after graduating, he ended up being my favorite professor in graduate school.

Looking back, I think my high school being so open, liberal, and caring perhaps made me think the rest of the world was this way too. We had a thriving gay / straight alliance and amazing guidance counselors, psychologists, and social workers who helped students who were having difficulties, and overall my school was a kind and welcoming place to be. My school was liberal to the point that the Westboro Baptist Church has come to protest my high school twice, once during a graduation and once during a random school day. Both times they were met with a "silent, not violent" counter-protest.

When I had a terrible cold followed by a sinus infection, and missed over a week of school, my teachers, guidance counselor, and parents had a meeting to discuss how best to support me in making up the work. No one said, "You have until tomorrow to turn in all of your papers, or you will fail the class."

On the second day of my sophomore year of high school, I somehow misread my schedule and thought my day started with a free period. I literally slept through my first class. Anyone who knows me will know that this is completely out of character for me, but these things happen. I came to school, realized my mistake, and went to my guidance counselor in tears. She was always helpful to me if I needed it and quickly took care of the problem.

I came to college thinking that people in power at institutions like schools cared for their students, provided guidance and help, and that schools had the interest of their students as the backbone of how they conducted themselves. If a high school guidance counselor could speak to a teacher to make sure that there are no ramifications for a student sleeping through a class, surely the Dean of a university could talk to a student's professors and make sure there are no consequences for missing class after being raped.

Though I had a decent time in high school being the speaker, I got to have the last word on my high school experience. A big part of my speech was how everyone had mispronounced my last name, but I didn't have the confidence to correct them. I spoke about my feelings of anonymity in high school and called out a teacher who repeatedly called me by the wrong first name, Katherine. My message was to stand strong as the person you are and not let anyone call you the wrong name or make you feel less than anyone else. I got a standing ovation and when I went up for my diploma, everyone that I shook hands with raved about my speech.

The teacher I called out had missed graduation, but heard about my speech and sent me the nicest email to apologize. It had not really occurred to me to consider his feelings and I was embarrassed. I didn't respond. After I graduated from college, I was reminiscing about high school with my friend, Clara. I told Clara about the email and she was adamant that I needed to respond. The next day, I sent my teacher an email saying how sorry I was for calling him out in the speech and for not responding in the first place. I think maybe responding after all that time was more awkward than not responding at all, but I guess best practice is to always respond, especially if someone is apologizing to you. He sent me an email a few days later that basically said "no hard feelings." It's amazing (sad) that my high school teacher sent me an email to apologize after I publicly outed him for making an honest mistake, yet I will never get an apology from anyone at my college for pushing me to the brink of suicide.

Anyway, let's get back to what happened when I tried to be the speaker in college. The process to be the student speaker was much like it had been in high school. I drafted my speech in my creative writing journal and wrote from my heart. I emailed the committee my speech and was asked to come in and audition. My audition was a few days later in the Student Center. I had only been there a few times since freshman year. I lived in an apartment, so I didn't need to go there for food and mail and there were no more hearings. It felt strange to be back there in the building where so many horrible things had happened, but I pushed through and my audition had gone perfectly. I thought I had it in the bag. A few days later, I got an email to say that they had chosen someone else.

But how was that possible? I had convinced myself that this would make things right. I was given a final chance to prove everyone wrong. Who I needed to prove wrong at this point, I'm not sure. Remember literally no one involved with my case still worked at this school, but still I had a sick feeling about the whole thing. My grades weren't enough. Changing the letter in my file was not possible. I wanted to feel like I had in high school and have the final word on my college experience, but in a way I'm glad I wasn't the speaker. My graduation was really early in the morning and I would have had to get up even earlier to be the speaker. Being the speaker also would have given me a false sense of victory and closure. I did not need to be the speaker to own my college experience and I didn't need to prove anything to anyone.

I'm sure it was amazing when the girl who was chosen gave her speech, but I was just too upset to pay attention. When I went up to get my diploma (or actually the empty frame they give you, as your real diploma isn't ready yet), I handed my notecard to the man reading off the names and people's honors. Everyone had had to write a notecard with the correct pronunciation of their name and what honors they were graduating with, if any. Mine read: Lory Kates, Summa Cum Laude. Only the man read it as, Lory Kates, Magna Cum Laude. I paused on the stage and angrily whispered to him, "Summa, it's Summa Cum Laude."

The man said, "Oh, sorry, Summa Cum Laude," and then repeated, "Summa Cum Laude," to the crowd. He seemed annoyed to be corrected, as there were a lot of students to get through, but no way had I worked that hard to not get my moment at graduation. I walked across the stage, not noticing what I was doing or whose hand I was shaking. All that work, the all-nighters, making myself go to class on no sleep while fighting through my debilitating fear, and he had the nerve to say Magna.

I find it kind of funny now, how much I cared about grades – and that in the end, all that work just amounted to a few words on a notecard. All those years of work and struggle, and now college was over.

Here is the graduation speech that I wrote. Reading it now, it reminds me of how far I have come, and all that I still want to accomplish.

### Commencement Speech – 2015

*What if I told you that if you can wait for, and fight for, your chance to play with a plastic telephone – and if you can rebuild a tower of blocks – then you can wait for and fight for just about anything? My name is Laurie Katz and today I am going to prove just that.*

*As an early childhood education major, I've learned a lot from working with children. One day, I was observing a group of toddlers waiting to play with a toy telephone. A two-year-old girl sat patiently waiting her turn and whenever the phone became free a new child would swoop in and take the phone. I wanted to help this girl, but I also wanted to see how she would navigate this situation. Finally, when a boy who had just arrived on the scene went to grab the phone the girl turned to him and simply said, "No." I thought to myself, wow, we've all been dealing with this nonsense since we could barely talk.*

*I've seen countless children cry when they are unable to play with the toy they want to. We call these "minor disappointments", and in education classes we learn strategies on how to help children cope with them. That same devastation we felt at two when we couldn't play with the toy phone, we feel now when we don't get the job we wanted. Try telling a crying 22-year-old that what they are experiencing is just a "minor disappointment" and see how well that goes over.*

*When a child has their block tower knocked down, they cry. We felt that same devastation when a paper we thought we aced got torn apart. When a child rebuilds their tower it always comes out better than it was the first time they made it. And when we met with the professor and actually read the textbook, we got that A on our* next paper. We are primed at a young age to rise from sabotage and failure to make something better than we had before.

As we get older, the challenges grow as we grow. Learning to count to 100 was once as daunting as writing a 15-page research paper. If we didn't struggle, imagine how much harder life would be if the first time we faced challenges was after we graduated from college.

What we need to understand is that what we cry about today, we will laugh about tomorrow. We find it comical when a child gets upset over something we deem inconsequential, but one day getting job B when we wanted job A will seem as trivial as not getting that toy phone. And we will learn to either love job B or we will work harder to get the job we really wanted. As we get older there is more at stake in our disappointments, but there are also more rewards to our triumphs.

We've all waited for that plastic phone and we've all learned when to walk away and when to stand up for ourselves. I've had my block tower knocked down more times than I can count. We all have, and we are all better for it. We've learned when to rebuild and when to move on. If graduating from college was easy, would it feel this good?

Life is always full of challenges. The secret to being successful is using our inner and outer resources to meet and overcome them. At two it is having to fight for a plastic telephone. At four it is restarting your block tower. As we graduate at 22 or 30 or 50 or however old we are, it is restarting our lives. This school has given us all the building blocks we need to make this happen, but it is up to us how we are going to put them all together. We rebuilt our towers and we fought for that plastic phone, so we will take all the pieces given to us and we will fight for our futures. Congratulations class of 2015, I can't wait to see what we fight for!

# CHAPTER 27

## Present Day Laurie

Today it is May 7, 2017. I have been working on writing this since April 30. I currently have 27,476 words. I know I am not finished, but I like to think I'm getting close. I still have a notebook full of things to add and I need to edit what I have typed, but I have a good portion written and the ending is pretty set. I remember being shocked when I learned that TV shows and movies shoot scenes out of order, but in writing this it was easier to write the beginning and end and fill in the middle.

I woke up yesterday morning with my boyfriend and he went to the kitchen to unload the dishwasher, because he's amazing like that. So, I lay in bed listening to him put away the dishes and I marveled at my life. I went into the kitchen and we made breakfast together and then he headed out to visit his parents to help his mom with a project. I worked on writing this for a while and then I went on a long walk. It was warm and sunny and perfect.

After I had leftovers for dinner, my friend Clara came over. We were going to have a sleepover. We used to have them all the time before work and school and life got in the way. We walked to a restaurant in Boston for dessert. Clara and I love to go to this restaurant because the atmosphere is fun with chocolate themed décor that makes you feel like you are at

Wonka's factory. They also have the best food and desserts. It's the type of place that can make a salad unhealthy. Seriously, your salad will arrive on top of a waffle. Their food is good, but their desserts are amazing. Clara and I planned to go there for dessert and to catch up.

A couple weeks earlier, we had gone on a long walk around the city and I told her about what happened to me freshman year. I had told her tidbits of the story over the years, but she didn't realize the pieces were connected and I had never mentioned the rape.

"Wait, so the guy that you told me about who stalked you, he's the guy who ... you know, did that to you too?" she had asked me.

"Um, yeah, same guy. I don't even remember telling you about that," I responded.

"It was a while ago and you didn't say too much about it."

We walked for hours as I relayed the details that I never thought I would share with anyone. She was surprised, but supportive.

I had already told Kelly about writing this story, but I needed an outside opinion on it. I can't expect my therapist to give me an impartial view on therapeutic writing. As Clara and I walked to the restaurant, I told her that I was writing this story and she had a lot of questions.

"What do you want to do with your story? Like, do you want to get it published?" Clara asked.

"I literally have no idea. I just have to write it."

"I mean I haven't read it yet, but it's nearly impossible to get anything published."

"I know and I don't even know if it's any good. I just started and I couldn't stop."

"If you published it, then everyone would know what happened to you. I mean, it's your choice, just think about that."

"You're freaking me out. I just want you to read what I have so far and let me know what you think."

We got to the restaurant and our table was ready and waiting for us. I'm a planner, so we had a reservation. We ordered chocolate fondue, as we are slowly making our way through the dessert menu.

"Isn't it funny how when we hung out at college we went to bars and clubs and now we're getting chocolate fondue?" I said, when our fiery dessert arrived. We got cocktails too.

I'm 23, so I can do things like that.

We talked about our lives now and about how we met in high school. On the first day of freshman English we were partnered to interview each other. Almost 10 years later and our friendship is stronger than ever.

"You're in the story too," I told her, "but I changed your name to "Clara." The only name I didn't change is mine."

"Clara?"

"I can change it to something else, if you want me to."

"No, Clara is fine."

It was a total nostalgia night. We wanted to watch the first Twilight movie, as Twilight had been a huge part of our lives in high school. I hadn't been able to find my copy because I'm in the midst of moving but we were committed, so we left the restaurant and walked to the store. It started to pour on the way there and we just laughed about it. They had the movie and it was only five dollars, so we bought snacks as well.

We watched the movie while making commentary and reveling in how good it still is. We then settled on watching *Charmed*, another fandom that bonds us. I wanted Clara to read my story and she had said she would, but we were falling asleep on the couch. We went to bed, deciding it would be impossible to read until morning. In the morning, I made us breakfast and sat next to her at the table watching her read on my computer. I read along feeling like I needed to cringe.

When she got to the part about Sarah she said, "Is [blank] Sarah?"

"Yeah, remember I changed everyone's name but mine."

We ate eggs and I watched the pages scroll down. Clara made the occasional comment. "That Dean really was a piece of work."

After reading for a little over an hour, Clara had to leave, but she read most of what I have so far.

"I know I can't be impartial because I know you, but so far it's really powerful."

Maybe Clara wasn't the impartial reader that I was looking for, but it felt good to have one person read part of this. We hugged goodbye and Clara headed out.

My boyfriend was supposed to be home in the late afternoon, but he came home early, and it was the best surprise to see him at the door. We went on a walk in the May sunshine along the river, holding hands as we always do. Sailboats drifted by and we watched a group of yellow, downy baby geese munch on the grass. Our walk was cut short due to my blisters from my extreme amount of walking the day before, so we drove to the supermarket to get dinner supplies. We made salmon for dinner and then lay on the couch. Being with my boyfriend has made me happier than I thought possible.

In the spring of 2016, after being in therapy for a year, I felt ready to start dating. I decided to make a profile online and I discussed this with Kelly. On my first day on the site I found my boyfriend, so I probably don't have the most relatable online dating experience. A week later we had our first date.

From the start we took things slowly. One night, maybe a month or so into us dating, I started crying when we were kissing. I told him that something had happened to me, but I wasn't ready to tell him about it yet. He was understanding and it made me trust him more. I think we had been dating for about four months when I told him about being raped. We were lying on his couch and I told him I had something I had to tell him. I had discussed this a lot with Kelly and the timing felt right. Still, I was worried that knowing what happened to me would make him not want to be with me anymore. This seems so ridiculous to me now, but back then it was a real concern. When I told him, he listened to my story and held me when I cried. He told me how sorry he was for what I went through and that it didn't change the way he felt about me.

Consent is a part of our relationship and it's a two-way street. When we first starting dating, this included asking each other if it was okay to hold hands and cuddle. For other things we still ask each other if this is okay and we are sure to stop immediately if either of us is uncomfortable. Being in therapy throughout our relationship has helped me understand my reactions and to gear up for difficult conversations. Debriefing with Kelly has helped me to figure out what works and what doesn't work and being with my boyfriend is everything I ever hoped for myself.

Now it is 10:46 at night. One of my cats, a big fluffy guy named Blue, is pawing at me because I'm not giving him enough attention and I need to get ready for bed. I do not know why I'm writing this, but I hope someday it will help someone and make them not feel alone. Yes, I'm afraid of people's reactions. I'm afraid everything I did will be judged and torn apart. I'm afraid that people will think all the things I thought for so many years, that it was my fault and that I made all the wrong choices. But just maybe if you've read my story you'll understand how trauma affects people, about the flaws in the systems we have that are supposed to help people, and that the only person at fault for a rape is the rapist.

I hope that I can help people and that they will relate to what I went through and just maybe they'll feel less alone and realize they're not at fault.

My life is not perfect. I am in debt from student loans and I always buy the store brand. I still have the rare panic attack and occasional trouble sleeping, but I'm alive and I love my life. I never thought I could have the life that I have now, and I never thought I would find love. Rape does not ruin your life forever.

# CHAPTER 28

## Final Thoughts

There's something that I did not include when originally writing this book and it is this: on that night, Noah orally raped me. I really did not want to include this. I agonized over whether to include it for months and after many discussions with Kelly and Clara, I have decided that if I am going to do this, I want to include everything. Because the things that are hard for me, or embarrassing, or that I struggle with, are the things that I need to share. Because if someone out there is struggling with this too, I don't want them to feel alone or that they did anything wrong.

I think I can truly say I know being raped was not my fault. I think I can also say that being orally raped was not my fault, but this is something a bit different. I don't think my mind let me make a complete memory of this, but I have glimpses of what happened, and of doing what I had to do to give myself a shot of making it out of that bedroom alive. Because when you go through a trauma like that, your body does what it has to, to keep you from dying.

For years I felt so responsible. There's a difference (or at least I thought there was) between having someone hold you down, and force themselves into you, and having someone push you onto your knees to force themselves into your mouth. I felt so complicit in this part of that night, because I had to be an "active" participant. It's hard for me to pinpoint exactly when this happened during my time in Noah's bedroom, but that's just how my memory processed the trauma. I just know it happened and that it made me disgusted with myself.

Oral rape is so difficult to come to terms with, because I was a part of it. I still struggle with this more than other things, so I feel it's important to talk about, because if I'm struggling, maybe other people are too. There is no one at fault for oral rape, other than the rapist. No one. It doesn't matter if you sucked them or touched them, if you didn't consent, you didn't consent. Threats or implied threats and overwhelming fear have forced you to do something you didn't consent to.

When I was in Noah's bedroom after he went to greet my friends, I felt something in my mouth and I put my fingers in to pull it out. It was a black pubic hair. I couldn't get it off my hand fast enough. I wiped it off on his bed and went to the bathroom to wash my hands, wash my mouth out with soap, find something to clean myself off with, and eventually to throw up. The image of that pubic hair on my hand is something I wish I could forget. I wish I could tell you I'm 100% recovered, and these things don't bother me. But I also think it's okay to not be 100% okay and to still be working through some things.

I was in denial for a long time about being raped, but this part of that night took me significantly longer to recognize and accept. It really wasn't until I had been out of college for a couple years that I even brought this up in therapy. None of it was my fault. And I feel stronger sharing this, because I did nothing wrong. Oral rape is still rape. There is nothing for me or anyone else to be ashamed of. Oral rape is still illegal and a felony. No matter what happened. No matter what you did. None of it was your fault.

I have accepted that whether I told Noah he could take my bra off or not I still would have been raped. Rape is not sex. People do not rape because they cannot control their sexual impulses, and that excuse that society affords them needs to stop. A girl should be able to tell a guy he can take her bra off and not be obligated to have sex with him. Maybe she changed her mind, maybe she had no intention of doing it in the first place. If she was drunk she can't consent anyway. It is still rape even if you do not say the exact words, "stop," or, "no" and you do not need to verbally say anything for a rape to still be just that. If someone stopped eating a cupcake after a bite, would you shove it in their face? And it is not just men that rape women, men can be raped too. Consent goes both ways.

Sometimes I have to remind myself that at 18 I was technically an adult, but looking back on it all I feel like I was still a child. I'm still struggling to not be ashamed, but there is such a social stigma associated with being raped.

*

I have guarded this as my darkest secret, telling few people, believing they will think less of me. About a year ago, I told my best friend from childhood, Emily, about what happened to me and it always amazes me to remember the incredible people in my life. Sometimes keeping something secret makes it bigger and scarier than if you share troubles with those you trust. It is your choice who you choose to disclose your life to and some people don't have the best reactions, but there are people who will support you.

This does not just happen to certain types of girls or just to girls in general. It is unfair that when people experience other traumatic events they can openly get support and talk about these events, but people with experiences like mine are shamed into silence. If he had mugged me, even if I had been drunk, I wouldn't feel as uncomfortable or embarrassed sharing this. Why is it that an assault is okay to talk about, but when you add the word, "sexual", you're just not supposed to say anything?

Victim blaming does not just apply to sexual crimes. I think it makes us feel some control over our lives. If we hear that someone died in a car accident, but they weren't wearing a seatbelt, it makes us feel safe. We always wear a seatbelt, so that could never happen to us. When my iPhone was stolen, multiple people assumed I had put my phone down on the bar. People probably thought, *I would never take my phone out and leave it anywhere, so that could never happen to me.* No, some a-hole just stole it right out of my bag. To stop theft, stop stealing. Bad things do happen, and we cannot always stop or control them, but we can be supportive and believe people when they do.

I was raped during the "red zone", which is the first six to eight weeks of a new school year at college. This is the time between the start of the school year and Thanksgiving and it is when 50% of sexual assaults occur, according to the Rape, Abuse & Incest National Network (RAINN). Schools are increasingly aware of this phenomenon and have increased training surrounding this time period, but so much of the training and rhetoric is for women and what they should do to keep themselves safe during this "dangerous time." If rape is no one's fault but the rapists, why are we warning young women to be more vigilant during this time and not directing this conversation to the whole student body? There is nothing about a student that makes them more "rapeable" during the first six weeks of school. We need to look at the perpetrators, not the victims, to see how we can stop these horrific crimes from continuing to happen. By continuing to accept that college rape is inevitable, we can never move forward. What we should be asking is, why are people coming to college and the first thing they do is make the choice to sexually assault someone?

Just think of Noah. Someone taught him how to read. They spent hours of their time being patient with him as he struggled to learn something we all take for granted. People loved him and cared for him. So much work goes into any person. He worked hard to graduate from high school and come to college. He was probably nervous to leave home and maybe he was even homesick. He was all these things and then he was a rapist. Why is this the case for so many rapists?

The idea of "date rape" or "acquaintance rape" is also harmful. A so called "rape" is what my idea of rape was – a guy you've never met grabbing you and raping you in an alley. If you know the perpetrator, or, let's say you're drunk and lay down in his bed, well then that's not "rape", that's "date rape." The problem with this is it makes the rape sound less serious and makes people feel a false sense of safety. There isn't some psycho running around raping people off the street, so I'm safe. The thing is the vast majority of rapes are "date rapes". To me, let's just call it rape. Why do we need to qualify it? Why does it need to have some extra word that seems to only put more blame on the victim? She was on a date. She knew him. She willingly went with him. He still raped her. And I apologize that my phrasing often includes a female victim and male rapist. I know that sexual assaults are perpetrated against men and that this is just as devastating. My experience was of a man raping me, so I am writing from that viewpoint.

Rape culture or the normalization of rape is disturbingly widespread, and so much of what we do to "prevent" rapes is born from this mindset that rape is inevitable. So much of the rhetoric about campus rape or rape in general is "don't drink, and if you do, watch your drink. Always walk home with a friend, and carry pepper spray." Yes, always be as careful as you can, but how's this anti-rape rhetoric? Don't rape. It's that simple. Stop putting the burden of preventing sexual assault and the blame on the victim. And maybe when we start taking these crimes seriously, having genuine conversations about consent, and holding the perpetrators accountable these crimes will stop.

What happened to me could have happened at any college. Change is needed around the globe and about one quarter of rapists will reoffend. If you do not want rape to tarnish the reputation of your college, expel rapists. Take a stand that your school takes these crimes seriously. Rape at colleges and rape in general does not have to be a reality that we accept.

Someone raped me. That's on him. My university failed me, and I may never understand why they made the judicial case against me. Is it really easier to believe that someone would pretend to be raped than that it actually happened? Or, did they just want to silence me?

Eventually, I was encouraged to go to the police, but this was months after I had been told not to "waste their time". I should explain that this was only after my dad came to Chicago and I firmly believe that the Dean was trying to cover his ass. By the time I went to the police, I was told too much time had passed and there was nothing they could do. At my hearing one of the pieces of "evidence" against me was that I hadn't gone to the police until months later. Looking back on everything now, it feels orchestrated. Maybe it would have been "too late" even two weeks after I was raped, but I think that, even then, something could have been done.

During my time in college I am sure other people had to go through what I went through. One case even became big enough (probably because it involved a student athlete) that people found out about it and had some strong reactions, but this died down after a few days. During one of my meetings with the Dean, I asked him how many cases he heard that were like mine. He said at least one a term. That's a person choosing to sexually assault another human being, and this is happening at least once every 10 weeks. I'm sorry, I mean *allegedly* choosing to sexually assault another person. Allegedly. And that's just one school. I feel I should note that according to Rape Victims Advocates, only between 2% and 8% of rapes are falsely reported. The same percentage as other felonies.

Schools need to change dangerous policies that are created to decrease liability and really just harm students. I didn't return to my dorm to safety that night because I was afraid of getting in trouble for underage drinking. Later during my freshman year, I got horrible food poisoning and spent the night in my dorm's bathroom. An RA was alerted to my plight and said he would need to call an ambulance. Through vomit and tears I begged him not to. I had food poisoning for fuck's sake, and I didn't want people to think I'd been drinking underage. After a long debate, he begrudgingly let it go.

I used to visit my sister when she was in college during my spring break. I noticed that on the door of my sister's room there was a poster that explained what to do if you were sexually assaulted. I never thought it could happen to me, so I never took the time to really read it, but perhaps if something like that had been available to me I would have been better educated about my options. And to have such a poster shows that a school takes this matter seriously. At the end of the hearing, I told the Vice President of Student Affairs that they should add posters such as these to the dorms when she asked me *again*, "if there's anything else you'd like to share with me." I explained the posters and how they would be helpful. She had no response. I told myself before the hearing that this was the one thing I had to be sure I said to her and by the end of the meeting I figured I had nothing left to lose. Clearly, the school had no interest in admitting that rapes happen.

I know that things have changed since 2011, and sexual assault is being brought to light more and more, but there is still so much work left to be done. I have spent years poring over articles, hearing news stories, and watching TV shows that try to make sense of society's reaction to these crimes. From my experience and those of others, I have some requests. Stop normalizing that rape is inevitable. Stop normalizing that perpetrators will not be held accountable. Stop normalizing suicide after rape. Normalize therapy and medication. Normalize that schools and judges and the public believe victims. Most of all, we need to normalize the idea that you can live a normal life after being raped.

All I can do is continue living my life and work hard for myself, not to prove anything to anyone else. Yes, I said those 10 words and it does not matter. I no longer blame myself for what happened. I am stronger than I ever thought I could be. It was not my fault.

"At least one a term." I am sure there are so many more cases that the Dean never heard, and maybe no one has heard. I hear you. I am so sorry for what you went through. It was not your fault. Your feelings are valid. Your pain is valid. You owe it to yourself to get help. I will not tell you that you have to go to the police or anything like that. Whatever you do is your choice. Just know that there are people who will believe you and you are stronger than this. We all heal differently, and you will heal. I believe you.

Here is the new ending to the story I wrote in creative writing. Lindy no longer commits suicide.

*Lindy would think back on that night and remember that it was just that, one night in her life. It had been terrifying, but she was still alive and her life was too precious to give up. When Lindy was driving or doing the dishes she might think, I was raped. And the words would feel foreign to her, like she needed to remind herself that this had happened, when for so many years the words "rape victim" had been the only words she could identify with. Suicide would be a very real option for her for a while. It would taunt her as a way out, but it was a lie. She had control over her life by living it, not by dying. She would imagine sometimes finding out that Noah had been arrested for some other crime, as he would never be held accountable for his actions that night. But to imagine this was to wish what he had done to her on someone else, and she could not do that. No, she would live her life like any other person and learn how to trust and love. The dark wouldn't terrify her anymore and she would learn how to accept what had happened and feel no shame or guilt. The years would go by and every minute it would hurt less, until there she would be, driving in her car on her way home from work and she would remember what had happened, like she was remembering being caught in a bad storm. She was alive and that's all life can ask from any of us.*

If you are affected by any of the issues mentioned in this book, we encourage you to seek help and support.

www.rapecrisis.org.uk
0808 802 9999

www.rasac.org.uk
01962 868 688

Readers in the US can contact RAINN, or the National Sexual Assault Hotline on 800 656 4673.

# ACKNOWLEDGEMENTS

This book would not have been possible without the bravery of so many survivors. It is from your actions that I was able to break my silence. Whether you have disclosed your assault or not, your story has immense value and I thank you for your courage and resilience.

I would like to thank my friends who supported me in this process and pushed me to make this book as open and honest as possible. I thank my amazing boyfriend, Rob, who has been with me every step of the way as my proofreader, shoulder to cry on, and best friend. And I thank my parents and sister for their love and support. I know this is the book you never wanted me to have to write.

I would like to thank my publisher, Trigger, for their belief in this book and for taking it beyond what I could have hoped for. Thank you to my editors, Kirsty Reade and Chris Lomas, who put up with constant additions and treated this book with care and sensitivity. I thank the whole team at Trigger, not just for their work on my book, but for helping mental health struggles no longer be hidden.

Finally, I thank the 18-year old girl who endured a horrible act of violence and fought for me to have the life I have today. This book helped me reclaim my voice and take ownership of my story. I am so grateful to be alive.

**If you found this book interesting ...
why not read these next?**

# Teacup in a Storm

## Finding my Psychiatrist

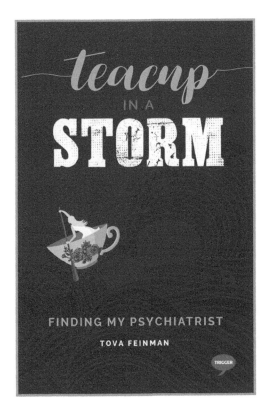

Wracked with trauma from childhood abuse, Tova sought therapy to soothe her mind. However, it is not as easy as simply finding a person to talk to ...

# Must Try Harder

## Adventures in Anxiety

After 30 years hiding in the shadows, beset by extreme social anxiety, Paula McGuire decided to change her worldview – one terrifying and exhilarating challenge at a time. In this book, Paula shares her extraordinary journey from recluse to adventurer.

# Stronger, Braver, Wiser

## How My #MeToo Story Helped Me Thrive

*Stronger. Braver. Wiser.* follows Jennifer Potter as she battles the highs and lows involved in taking her abuser to court.

the *Shaw* mind
FOUNDATION

Creating hope for children,
adults and families

Sign up to our charity, The Shaw Mind Foundation
**www.shawmindfoundation.org**
and keep in touch with us; we would love to hear
from you.

*We aim to bring to an end the suffering and despair caused
by mental health issues. Our goal is to make help and support
available for every single person in society, from all walks of
life. We will never stop offering hope. These are our promises.*

# www.triggerpublishing.com

Trigger is a publishing house devoted to opening conversations about mental health. We tell the stories of people who have suffered from mental illnesses and recovered, so that others may learn from them.

**Adam Shaw** is a worldwide mental health advocate and philanthropist. Now in recovery from mental health issues, he is committed to helping others suffering from debilitating mental health issues through the global charity he co-founded, The Shaw Mind Foundation. www.shawmindfoundation.org

**Lauren Callaghan** (CPsychol, PGDipClinPsych, PgCert, MA (hons), LLB (hons), BA), born and educated in New Zealand, is an innovative industry-leading psychologist based in London, United Kingdom. Lauren has worked with children and young people, and their families, in a number of clinical settings providing evidence based treatments for a range of illnesses, including anxiety and obsessional problems. She was a psychologist at the specialist national treatment centres for severe obsessional problems in the UK and is renowned as an expert in the field of mental health, recognised for diagnosing and successfully treating OCD and anxiety related illnesses in particular. In addition to appearing as a treating clinician in the critically acclaimed and BAFTA award-winning documentary *Bedlam*, Lauren is a frequent guest speaker on mental health conditions in the media and at academic conferences. Lauren also acts as a guest lecturer and honorary researcher at the Institute of Psychiatry Kings College, UCL.

Please visit the link below:

**www.triggerpublishing.com**

Join us and follow us...

@triggerpub

Search for us on Facebook